TAX LIEN AND TAX DEED INVESTING

The Proven Technique

THOMAS J. SENATORE

ISBN 978-1-0980-0604-4 (paperback)
ISBN 978-1-0980-0605-1 (digital)

Christian Faith Publishing, Inc.
832 Park Avenue
Meadville, PA 16335
www.christianfaithpublishing.com

Printed in the United States of America

Contents

Introduction

Tax sales have been around for hundreds of years in Europe and have been in the United States for almost two hundred years, and yet it is still a relatively unknown strategy for investors. Tax lien sales and tax deed sales have gained more notice in the United States over the past ten to twelve years due to the introduction of online auctions where you no longer need to be on the courthouse steps to play in this game. Although a few large corporations still participate in the auctions, most bidders are small groups of locals that actively pursue this area of investing.

I discovered this investing technique in 1997 while employed as a paralegal for the Law Firm of Allocca and Pellegrino, PC, located in Parsippany, New Jersey. For nearly two years, I studied the tax foreclosure process under the guidance from the two partners of the firm, Michael Pellegrino, Esq., and Ralph Allocca, Esq., and also learned from our clients in order to develop my own strategy and twist to this well-kept secret.

I also studied the different real estate investing techniques taught by Russ Whitney and Robert Kiyosaki to combine what I learned in order for me to find my niche in the tax lien and tax deed investing. I found that while many investors in the area of tax liens and tax deeds like to keep this area secret, many others were willing to teach me such as a gentleman named Bob Delvecchio. The knowledge he imparted as well as from many others helped me to become the successful investor I am today. During my journey I have been a national speaker and trainer on tax lien investing traveling the different markets teaching strategies of real estate investing. Since 2009 I have taken this unique concept of investing to markets around the world places such as London, New Zealand, Australia, Malaysia, Singapore, Indonesia and China where I have shared my experiences with tens of thousands of investors.

There are over 7500 tax sales each year of which there are over 1,500,000 tax liens and tax deeds sold in the different states during the year of which you, the investor, can take advantage. There are tax lien sales and tax deed sales, and you need to determine which one works best for you. You need to learn the process in your state and determine if you are in a tax lien state, tax deed state, or both.

As you decide to purchase the liens or deeds, you need to have a good attorney to complete the foreclosure on your behalf. I will explain how to assemble your team and surround yourself with individuals that will help you make money using this technique. Many investors have heard of buying tax liens or tax deeds, and how many have made hundreds to thousands to millions of dollars with this technique?

While there are stories of properties purchased for a few hundred dollars and sold for tens of thousands of dollars, they are true, but they are not the normal transaction. I have even heard of a national speaker tell the group that you can buy properties for pennies on the dollar and that it is guaranteed by the government; I am here to tell you they *do not* guarantee anything. As a matter of fact, they announce a disclaimer prior to the start of the sale. What they do guarantee is that if a homeowner pays the delinquent amount to the tax collector, the tax collector will then pay the investor the amount of the lien plus interest.

Each of the fifty states has different rules based on their statutes of which we have researched for you and have for your reference in this book. For example, in Texas, which is a tax deed state with redemption, the homeowner pays the investor the full tax amount plus a 25% penalty. Be sure you check the rules of your state before you invest as there are many ways you can make a lot of money, but if you're not careful, you may lose money.

Read this book carefully to understand the difference between a tax lien sale and a tax deed sale, and then take your first step to become a knowledgeable investor. You will then become the knowledgeable investor and lower the risk associated with investing. Then and only then will you be on the road to financial independence.

I dedicate this book to my wife, Cindy Fay-Hamilton, who not only helped encourage me to write this book but is also my best friend. Without her encouragement and conviction to push me to write this book, I would not have finished this and would like to say thank you. In addition, my baby sister, Linda Vecheski, and grandfather, James Schiavone, who have gone and always believed in me and pushed me to excel in everything I did, I say thank you. I would also like to thank some of the many family and friends who have supported me through the years of which without them, I would not be the person who I am today. My mom, Dolores Senatore, as well as our five children, Garrett, Jonathan, Terry, TJ, and Meredith, all of which have had an impact on my life. My close friends, Dallas Peltz, Bob Baier, and A. C. Johnson, to name a few, thank you all for your support and for never stopping in believing in me!

CHAPTER 1

Tax Lien Basics

The collection of taxes goes back as far as one can remember and was used to pay for the services provided by the governing body. Today, we use these taxes as a way for the community to pay for the services such as the police department, fire department, schools, sanitation department, and department of public works, city government, government buildings, and more. If the tax collectors did not collect all the taxes that were due from the homeowners, then the tax collectors would not have enough money in their accounts to pay for the services mentioned above that they provide for the community.

There are stories that I heard where people as far back as to the early 1900s were able to buy property for the taxes owed because the owner could not pay for them. Since the beginning of the collection of taxes, the tax collector would always have some people that did not pay their property taxes for one reason or another, and, therefore, the tax collector had to find a way of encouraging the property owner to make the payments. They also had to find a way to get the homeowners pay the delinquent taxes in a fair manner as the tax collector was an elected official and could not be reelected if they did not keep the homeowners' investment protected. Another obstacle the tax collector had to overcome was to devise a way in which to encourage others to pay the taxes on behalf of the owners where these others would benefit greatly while protecting the interest of the homeowners who elected these tax collectors. This became a problem for many states, and they had to find a way to enforce the collection of property taxes at the state level.

State laws, more commonly known as statutes, were passed by each state that gave the city or county tax collector the ability to sell off the delinquent taxes as a lien, or they could sell the property with a deed. The problem in this is that since each state passed its own laws or statutes on how the delinquent tax would be sold off, there became fifty-one different varieties of tax sales. You may ask how can there be fifty-one different varieties of tax sales if there are only fifty states. Well, Washington, DC, has its own set of rules as well. Not only does DC have their own way of selling off the delinquent taxes, they even offer a free class to all of those who wish to attend and buy at their sale. We will cover the tax lien sales first, and then we will explain tax deed sales.

The first and most common method of collecting property taxes are by way of tax lien sales. This is where the city or county tax collector would sell by open public auction to a third party (you, the investor) the delinquent taxes at a tax lien sale, and the document you would get is called a tax sale certificate or a tax lien certificate depending on which state you're in. This sale is done after the tax collector had tried over a specific period of time to get the homeowner to pay the delinquent taxes owed. This incentive for the person buying the tax sale certificate (or actually loaning money to the taxing authority on behalf of the property owner) is that are entitled to earn interest on the amount they paid for the tax sale certificate. Think of this like a savings bond that you buy and have to wait several years before you can cash it in. You don't get any money on a monthly basis, but your investment grows on a monthly basis, which is what a tax lien does. This interest can range from 8% to 50% per year depending on which state you're investing in. The method in which the tax collector sells the tax sale certificate also will vary and will be discussed in detail later on in this book.

Now that the tax collector had the means to enforce the collection of taxes, this would cause the tax collector to follow many rules, and for this reason, many cities and counties did not sell these tax liens right away. In some states, there are tax liens held by the tax collector that were over forty years old as I found in a small town in New Jersey called Westwood. This type of investing in tax liens and tax deeds was passed many years ago but only became popular in the past ten to fifteen years. Most of the tax lien sales had a small attendance of one to three people, and in some instances, the tax collector would be the one buying the liens (this is where the city or county held liens began). The tax sales from the 1980s to the late 1990s have been attended by only a few investors. That number has increased over the years, and now, you can have anywhere from ten to one thousand bidders at these sales.

With the tax lien sale, if the property is not sold off to the public, it is then sold to the city or county for the face amount with the maximum amount of interest permitted by law. The city or county then has the ability to complete its own foreclosure against the owners and lien holders in what is called an *in rem* foreclosure. The tax lien certificates usually have to be held for two years such as in New Jersey, but when the tax collector takes the tax lien certificate, they will start the *in rem* foreclosure after the certificate is only six months old. The *in rem* foreclosure usually takes six to eight months, and then the city or county can sell off the property for a profit. Most states have the tax lien sale once a year, and the interest on the certificates range from 10% per year to 20% per year. Most tax liens have to be held by the purchaser for two years on average, and after the two years, they have the right to start a foreclosure action to get the title to the property they have paid the taxes on.

Once you have purchase a tax lien, you must now follow the state statutes on how long the certificate must be held before the foreclosure process can be started. This is what we call the redemption period, and this is for an average of two years. The redemption period is set up to allow the homeowner the opportunity to save their property from being taken away from them in foreclosure for nonpayment of property taxes.

Remember that the tax laws were created to protect homeowners, and if they did not give the homeowner the ability to save their home, the people who created these laws would find themselves out of a job. The time period that a tax sale certificate must be held before the holder can apply for a tax lien foreclosure will vary from one year to three years. In the majority of states, it is two years or twenty-four months before the foreclosure process can be started, and then it takes about another nine months to complete the foreclosure process. All during this time, the property owner has had the chance to redeem the tax lien and keep his home. After the foreclosure is completed, you now own the property and can either keep it, rent it, or sell it, whatever you want because now you are the legal titled owner.

Tax Lien Foreclosure Process

The foreclosure process for tax liens is complex and should be completed by an attorney who understands the procedures of a tax lien foreclosure. If you attempt this by yourself, which you are permitted to do under the laws of our country, you must be sure that you do not make a mistake or miss out on a time limitation or you can lose your entire investment. I cannot emphasize enough on how important it is to have the foreclosure process performed by an attorney. I, myself, being a paralegal who worked on tax lien foreclosure from start to finish, do not do my own tax lien foreclosures. It was something I learned while going through my training as a paralegal that it is not wise to represent yourself in court, and I agree that when it comes to tax lien foreclosure and my money is at stake, I will not take the chance of doing something wrong. I will cover briefly the basic procedure for a tax lien foreclosure from the date that the tax lien is sold at a public auction till you get the deed to the property.

Once you have reviewed the process, you will see why it is so important to consult an attorney who specializes in tax lien or tax deed foreclosures. The tax collector holding the tax sale must be advertised in the local newspaper at least twenty-one days before the sale. This is usually placed in the legal section or the classified section of the local newspaper in that county. The newspaper notice will include the name of the property owner, address of the property, tax identifier of the property, and the amount of the taxes that are delinquent. A written notice of delinquent taxes must also be sent to the property owners' last known address to allow them another opportunity to pay off the delinquent taxes before the sale. The tax lien sales are open to the public, and they sell off each and every parcel that has a delinquent tax on it. At a tax lien sale, you bid the tax amount and the interest you would be willing to take. We will explain the bidding process in detail later, but for now, we will keep it basic, and all you need to know is that each person will bid down the percent interest rate till no one else bids a lower percentage interest rate.

The lowest bidder will have to complete some paperwork for the tax collector such as an information sheet that will have your name in which the tax sale certificate will be issued to, your tax ID number, and a mailing address where you would like the certificate to be sent. At some of these sales, you may be required to preregister for the sale several days in advance of the sale or you may not be permitted to bid. Some tax collectors also require you to post 10% of your estimated purchases which means that if you plan on purchasing $10,000 in tax liens, you will need to deposit with the tax collector $1,000. If you end up buying more than $10,000, you may be required to post an additional deposit before you are permitted to bid on any additional liens. You need to keep in mind that this "tax sale certificate" is a lien on the property, and you need to understand that you do not own the property and that you do not have the right to go on the property or into the home. Usually, at the conclusion of the tax sale, you are required to pay for all of the tax sale certificates you purchased in full. The tax collector will tell the bidders at the conclusion of the sale what form of payment they will accept. Some tax collectors will permit personal checks or company checks, while others will insist on certified funds, wire transfers, or cash. Either way, you must pay for the tax sale certificate you won before the end of the day.

Once you receive the tax sale certificate, you must get it recorded in the county clerk's office or the Registrar of Deeds to protect your interest in the property. By doing this, you are informing all others that you have an equitable interest in the property and that if someone should try to foreclose the owner out of their rights to the property, they must inform you as well. If the owner tries to sell the property, your tax sale certificate will show up on the title search, and you usually will be paid at that time. The recording of the tax sale certificate is usually completed by your attorney, and there is a small recording fee that ranges from $10–$75 depending on your state. You now send a copy of the recorded tax sale certificate to the tax collector so they have a copy on file, and if the owner attempts to redeem (pay off the taxes due plus interest), they will notify you immediately. If the owner redeems after the foreclosure was started, then they will be required to pay the tax sale certificate dollar amount with the appropriate interest added as well as the legal fees for the foreclosure. From the time you buy the tax lien certificate to the time the foreclosure can be started varies from state to state.

There are currently twenty-five states that offer tax liens of which the top four tax lien states are Arizona which has a three-year redemption period, Florida, Illinois, and New Jersey. For the most part, the redemption period (the time in which the property owner can pay off the tax lien and keep from losing their property) is two years with the exception of Arizona, and it starts from the date the tax sale was held. One day after the two-year anniversary of your purchase of the tax lien certificate, you can start the foreclosure process. The foreclosure process is complex and is completed in several steps. This process takes an average of six to eighteen months to complete but can be longer if there are several owners to the property or if the owners have a common name.

We begin the process by having our attorney requesting a full title search on the property to determine all the parties that may have an interest in the property. The attorney will then create a list of defendants that will need to be served any and all notices and pleadings. (Pleadings is a legal term for any documents sent out relating to a court action.) The following list of pleadings will be explained in basic terms, and although they are similar for most states, they may be called by a different name. The first document of the litigation that is sent out is the thirty-day letter (see appendix 1), which is sent to all property owners and lien holders on the property. This is a notice that is mailed regular and certified mail to all of the defendants informing them that they have thirty days to pay off the tax lien amount to the tax collector or a foreclosure action will be filed against them. It advises them that they will be responsible for any and all legal fees if they do not pay off the entire amount including interest to the tax collector by the date specified in the letter. After the thirty days have lapsed, the attorney will then file the first legal document or pleading which is called a civil complaint for foreclosure (see appendix 2). This legal document will name all of the listed owners of the property as well as any lien or judgment holders found when the title search was performed.

The complaint and summons are served upon the defendants personally by a constable, sheriff's officer, or a process server. The complaint will list information such as when the plaintiff (investor) purchased the tax lien, the amount of the tax lien, interest of the tax lien, the defendants' name(s), the property address, and a legal description for the property. The summons (see appendix 3) will advise the defendants that they have been served regarding a court matter and that they need to file an answer in writing within thirty-five days, and it also encourages them to seek legal representation. The defendants will then have thirty-five days from the date they were served the foreclosure complaint and summons to respond by filing an answer. After the thirty-five days have lapsed for all the defendants, the attorney reviews the file to see if anyone filed an answer to the complaint.

If none of the defendants file an answer to the complaint, then the attorney will send to the courts a request for a notice of default (see appendix 4) for all of the defendants. This document is to notify the court that all of the defendants have been properly served and none of the defendants have filed and answer to contest the foreclosure.

The attorney then sends to the court a request for and order setting the time, place, and amount of redemption (OST) (see appendix 5). This document will be used to give the owner of the property one more chance to pay off the tax lien before they lose their legal rights to the property. This document will indicate the last date the owner can pay off the tax lien, the location of the tax collector, and the full amount needed to pay off the tax lien.

Once that date has lapsed, the attorney will send an affidavit of non-redemption (see appendix 6) to the tax collector who states that the tax collector was in their office on the date and time specified in the OST and that no person came in to pay that tax lien on that specific property.

This affidavit, plus a request for a final judgment (see appendix 7), is sent to the court as well as a certification of mailing to all defendants that the notice of default was served according to the rules of service. The court will review the entire package, and if all the documents are correct, the judge will sign the final judgment, and you are now the legal owner of that property. Many title companies will not insure your interest for sixty days because the courts have, from time to time, granted the rights of the property back to the owner if they come to the court with all the money needed to pay off the tax lien as stated in the OST. Either way, it does not matter because you still get all your principal and interest, you just did not get the big payday you had dreamed of.

When you get this final judgment back from the court, you must send it out to be recorded in the county clerk's office as your deed to the property.

Now that you have the final judgment, you are the legal owner of the property and now have the ability to go on the property and do whatever you like.

If there is a tenant in the property, you now can offer them a lease and collect rents. If they do not want to pay you rent, they have to leave, and if they refuse, you can evict them. Remember that since you own the property once the final judgment is issued, you *must* now get insurance on this property to protect your assets.

Tax Deed Foreclosure Process

In states like Florida which are hybrid states, they sell off the tax liens, and the tax collector will set up the tax deed sale only after a property has had a tax lien issued against it at least twenty-four months earlier.

The state offers the delinquent taxes to the open public once a year at a tax lien certificate sale which can take several days to complete.

The tax lien certificate is held for twenty-four months from the date the lien was applied to the property before the holder can request the tax lien be sold off as a tax deed.

In the state of Florida, the county will process the tax deed sale for the tax lien holder, and then the tax lien holder gets their money after the tax deed is sold off. The tax deed sales are held weekly in most counties around Florida as well in most states.

At the tax deed sale, the properties are sold off one by one. The highest bidder over the tax lien amount gets the tax deed to the property.

After the highest bidder pays in full the tax deed purchase, they now have to hire an attorney to perform a quiet title action (also known as quieting of the title).

This quiet title action is completed to ensure that all of the owners of the property or those with an interest in the property were properly notified by the county that the sale had taken place. After the quieting of the title has taken place, you now have "marketable" title to the property.

During the quieting of title, there is always a chance that the owner may be able to come back to claim their property. For that reason, it is suggested that you do not make any improvements on the property until that process is completed.

What can you do while you are waiting for the quieting of the title to be completed? Well, for one, you can collect the rents if the property is occupied. You can also place a tenant into the property if it is vacant. You may even want to move into the property yourself if this is part of your strategy. Don't forget that once you win the property at the tax deed sale, you are now the legal owner, and you now should get insurance on that property. You can go to the property to clean it up to increase the curb appeal to increase your marketability on the property and sell it for a profit.

There are some tax deed states where you get the title to the property, but you cannot enter the property because the owner has time to redeem the tax deed for several months. In Texas, if the property is owner occupied, the owner has twenty-four months to pay off the amount of the tax deed plus interest. During that time, if the owner does redeem the tax deed by sending the payment to the tax collector as required by the state statute, they must pay the tax collector a penalty of 25% of the amount you paid for the tax deed including the original amount of taxes that were owed. This penalty is annually, and the full amount is due at any time during the first year and not based on a per month amount.

An example would be the following. There is a tax of $1,000, and the property sells for $10,000. The owner comes in and pays the tax collector in fourteen months. Well, they first owe the $1,000 plus the 25% penalty on the bid amount of $10,000 ($2,500 penalty) for year one and a 25% penalty ($2,500 penalty) for year two which means they must pay the tax collector $6,000 ($1,000 for the tax + $5,000 for the penalty) of which the tax collector pays you $15,000 (your $10,000 bid + $5,000 penalty). In some counties in Texas, the owner is required to pay the purchaser of the tax deed the penalty amount and the taxes to the tax collector while the purchaser is then responsible to request his $10,000 bid amount from the tax collector as well. This is why Texas is such a desirable state to invest in tax deeds.

Most investors do not want the property but rather prefer to get the interest rate they can receive. A big attraction about Texas is that in this type of foreclosure, the "mineral rights" may be included in the sale, which would mean that any oil underground transfers with the tax deed sale. When there is a recorded long-term lease for the mineral rights, these mineral rights do not transfer to the winning bidder. How great would it be if the mineral rights were included in the tax deed sale and you end up with a property with oil under the soil?

State Procedure on Tax Sale Foreclosure

There are twenty-one states have tax lien sales:

Alabama
Arizona
Colorado
DC
Florida
Illinois
Indiana
Iowa*
Kentucky
Louisiana*
Maryland
Mississippi
Missouri
Montana
Nebraska
New Jersey
Oklahoma
South Carolina
South Dakota
West Virginia
Wyoming

These states usually have one sale a year, and each city or county gets to set the date for their sale. This will give you the ability to attend several sales in one state during the year. The states designated with a * after them indicate the states where you do not bid the interest rate down, but rather you bid down the percent of ownership you wish to receive. This is an odd way to have a sale since you could potentially end up with a 10% share of the property from a tax lien.

Once you do the foreclosure, you now own the property with the homeowner still holding the other 90% portion as tenants in common. You then would be required to force the sale and collect your share. In reality, the percent of ownership should not go much below 80%, and in some cases, the tax collector may offer the tax liens to the group by way of a lottery system. In this style, the tax collector would place each bidder's number in a container and pull one number out at a time. If the lucky bidder did not want that tax lien, the tax collector would draw another number until someone wanted that tax lien. If no one wanted that tax lien, then the tax lien certificate would then be sold off to the city.

There are twelve states that have tax deeds without a redemption period (no ability to get the property back) for owner:

Arkansas
California
Idaho
Kansas
Michigan
New Hampshire
North Carolina
North Dakota
Pennsylvania
Utah
Virginia
Washington

These states usually have one sale a month, and each city or county gets to set the date for their sale. This will give you the ability to attend several sales in one state during the year.

There are thirteen states that have tax deed sales with a redemption period (ability to get the property back) for owner:

Connecticut
Delaware
Florida
Georgia
Hawaii
Massachusetts
Nevada
New York
Ohio
Rhode Island
Tennessee
Texas
Vermont

These states usually have one sale a month, and each city or county gets to set the date for their sale. This will give you the ability to attend several sales in one state during the year. When a state gives the owner the ability to get the property back, they also give the investor the ability to make a profit if the owner does.

There are six states that have tax deed sales without redemption period (no ability to get the property back) for the owner; however, the opening bid for the property could be higher than the amount of the delinquent taxes owed:

Alaska	New Mexico
Maine	Oregon
Minnesota	Wisconsin

These states usually have one sale a month, and each city or county gets to set the date for their sale. This will give you the ability to attend several sales in one state during the year. When the tax collector sells off the property, they sever the owner's ability to get the property back, and the investor now has the ability to make a profit.

There are five states having both tax lien sales and tax deed sales:

Florida	tax liens, two-year redemption
	tax deeds, no redemption after QT
Massachusetts	tax liens, forty-two months
	tax taking, no redemption after QT
Nevada	tax liens, two-year redemption
	tax deeds, no redemption after sale notice
New York	tax liens, sold privately
	tax deeds, no redemption
Ohio	tax liens, two-year redemption
	tax deeds, no redemption

These are what I call the hybrid states because they incorporate both tax lien certificate and tax deed sales.

(State by state details can be found in chapter 7.)

Different Types of Auctions

There are several types of ways the tax collector can sell off the delinquent taxes. There are open bidding, sealed bidding, online bidding, round robin bidding, first to bid, taking, private, bulk, over the counter, and lottery, to name a few. The most common is the open bidding, and we will try to explain basically how each method is used and how to use this to your advantage.

Open bidding is the most common and is used throughout the United States. This type of sale is where all the bidders gather in one place to bid. This type of sale can be found in a courtroom of the township as in New Jersey or on the steps of the county courthouse as they do in Texas. In either case, they call out each individual parcel, and it is given to the winning bidder. If it is a tax lien sale, the lien is awarded to the person who is willing to accept the lowest amount of interest rate return per year. The interest rate typically starts anywhere from 8% as in Oklahoma to 24% as in Iowa. In some states like New Jersey, the bidding is very competitive, and the interest rate on most liens is bid down to zero, and then a premium bid is given. A premium bid is a dollar amount over the lien that the bidder will pay in order to win the bid. That means that they will get 0% interest on the tax lien amount plus they will get 0% interest on the additional money spent on the over bid.

Why would anyone do that? Well, let's see. Say one of the companies such as American Tax Funding wanted to buy a tax lien on a shopping center where the lien had a value of $87,000. The value of the shopping center was around $2 million dollars. They would calculate that the owner would probably redeem the certificate before they could foreclose on the property, and this would happen sometime between the sale and eighteen months. If they win the bid, they get a 6% penalty because the amount is over $10,000. What they would do is calculate the amount of outstanding taxes that could be paid to determine the maximum amount of the premium to allow them to get a minimum percent of profit. Let's say that there was an additional tax amount due over the tax lien sale in the amount of another $87,000. If they win the bidding, they automatically get to pay off the additional taxes (often called a subsequent tax) of $87,000 and at 18% interest on that money. So if the owner were to redeem the lien in thirty days, American Tax Funding would get back the initial lien of $87,000 with the 6% penalty which is $5,220 and the subsequent tax of $87,000 at an interest of 18% annually which is $1,305 for a total of $ 6,525 which is equal to 2.25% for the month or 27% over twelve months. If the lien were to be redeemed in the twelfth month, the yield would be as follows: the initial lien of $87,000 with the 6% penalty is $5,220, and the subsequent tax of $87,000 at an interest rate of 18% annually is $15,660 for a total of $17,270, which is equal to 9.9% for twelve months. If it were to be redeemed in the eighteenth month, the return would be as follows: the initial lien of $87,000 with the 6% penalty is $5,220, and the subsequent tax of $87,000 at an interest rate of 18% annually is $23,490 for a total of $26,100, which is equal to 15% for the eighteen months. A company like American Tax Funding spends approximately $40,000,000 in New Jersey and, with that return, would make approximately $6,000,000 of which it probably cost them half for the use of the money.

That is why you may see the big companies bid the large premiums at the sale because they have calculated the profits with different numbers to see what is the most they can bid and still make good profits. If we use their system against them, we would know that they have to bid on the higher dollar value liens and that they most likely would not be interested in the smaller liens of say $800 and lower. If we, as the small-time investor, were to target these liens, we would not have as much competition and could consistently get the tax liens at 18% and in the end get a much better return than the large companies.

In May of 2006, I attended the Collier County, Florida, tax sale which took approximately three days to sell off all of the tax liens. Prior to the sale, the tax collector, Guy Carlton, had a mini seminar on what to expect from his tax sale and what he would tolerate and what he would not tolerate. This event took approximately ninety minutes and for the most part was informative, but for the novice, he basically scarred them to not even attending the sale. The meeting room where the sale was conducted was filled to capacity, and there were over one hundred preregistered bidders in attendance.

The room was comprised mostly with local individuals whom I observed were there to see what was going on as well the large corporations who were present and were bidding aggressively. Out of all those in attendance, there were approximately thirty to forty active bidders which were great for those bidding as they won many tax liens. I was there for the first two hours and was able to purchase fifteen tax liens at 18% each, while the large corporations were getting all of 1/4 of a percent.

Although I only spent a few thousand dollars that day, I could have easily spent $50,000 to $100,000 and have earned 18% on my tax liens. The large corporations on their purchases will only earn a maximum of 5% over the life of the lien up till seven years, while I will earn 18% per year.

So how was I able to beat the big guys, and what was my secret to earning an 18% return? I went to the sale with the intention of bidding all the tax liens that were under $800 which are the smaller tax liens that the local guys would bid on and the big guys would probably not bid on, and I was correct. The way it worked was that when the big guys did not bid, the small guys would bid, and they would not bid down the interest rate, and the tax collector would then pick someone to award the tax lien to at 18%.

Sealed bidding is where the bid is mailed to the taxing authority by a specific date and opened on the date and time specified by the taxing authority. In some cases, there can be open bidding and sealed bidding at the same sale for a specific sale. What will happen is that once the open bidding concludes for that specific parcel, the tax collector will then open all the sealed bids to see if the sealed bids are at a better offer then the open bids.

This process is used more likely for the tax deed sales where you bid up the price of the property. The minimum bid is established by the amount of the back taxes that are due, and then you send in a bid amount above that. There are some instances where the opening bid could be less than the amount of the taxes owed, but this is not common. If this is a tax lien sale and they are bidding down the interest rate, they look to see if the sealed bid is for a lower interest rate then shouted out at the open sale. If the tax lien sale is for an amount above the interest (premium bidding), then the tax collector will see if the sealed bids are for a value greater than the value shouted out at the open sale. I am sure you get the point of how this works.

Online bidding is where the tax collector uses the Internet to sell off the delinquent taxes. This system is similar to eBay in which you make offers and see if someone outbids you. There will be a date and time when the sale is closed, and no more bids will be permitted. There are several states that have started to go to the online bidding due to the number of bidders that the sale attracts, of which what has been used in Orange County, Florida.

In most cases, you will need to be preregistered before the sale starts and open an account so you can bid. You will also need to open up an account to hold your bidding funds, and they usually require that you have 10% or more of you total purchase in your funds account so you can bid. An example would be they require 10% in the account before you can bid and you have $1,000 in the account. You will now be able to bid on properties up to $10,000; if you have already won properties that total $9,500, you can only bid on properties up to $500 as you would have used up $950 of funds in your account. Some of the online bidding is done live where you need to be on the computer and bid as the property is offered for sale.

Other types of sales could be where you set a minimum and maximum bid price and the highest bid value wins once the auction time is set.

Round robin bidding is where the tax collector will offer the first person in the room the property, and if they do not want the property, that individual will pass, and it is then offered to the next person. This process continues until someone takes the property, and if no one wants that property, the tax collector will strike it off to the tax collector. This means that if no one wants the property, it will then be sold back to the tax collector for the amount of taxes owed. At this point, the property goes into a "Lands Available" department of the tax collector where you can buy the properties directly without any competition. This system or process usually is agreed to in advance by all of those in attendance at the sale. This type of sale does not happen too often, and it usually must be agreed to by all those in attendance at the sale. The great thing about having this type of sale is that you have a very good chance of getting several tax liens at the full interest rate and not have to compete with others. The downside is that if you are there for a particular tax lien that the odds are not in your favor, you will be offered that tax lien on the property when it is sold.

First to bid is where the property is sold to the first person who yells out the amount of tax owed. In the states where this program is used, there is not a lot of competition, and there may be only a handful of people in attendance. The way this process works is where the property for sale is announced, and each person who wants this property yells out, and the tax collector awards that property to that person. If more than one person yell out, the tax collector then has to determine who was the first to yell out or have them choose who gets the property.

Tax taking of the tax lien or deed is where the tax collector takes all of the delinquent taxes to foreclose in rem so they can sell the property themselves. The tax collector will buy the entire sale instead of selling to a group of individuals. This is great for the tax collector as they do not have to spend the time running a sale or deal with all the paperwork associated with a typical sale where there may be several hundred certificates issued and twenty to forty investors or more. They now own the certificates and can now do a quick tax lien foreclosure and then sell the properties after they get the ownership and keep the profits.

Private sales are where the tax collector will sell off the tax liens or deeds to a private group. What this is defeats the open competition as the tax collector sells the liens or deeds to an individual or a small group that were there by invitation only. This does not happen too often, but when it does, it is great to be part of that special group.

Bulk sales are where the tax collector offers the entire portfolio of the uncollected taxes for that city or county for sale to the open public, but instead of selling each parcel individually, they sell the entire group as a single transaction. This is great logistically for the tax collector as they are required to keep track of the buyers for each sale they hold, and as they have only one bidder, this becomes very simple to do. One of the major disadvantages is that you now need to have access to a lot of money in order to bid at these sales. Most tax collectors will require the bidders to post a substantial bond or deposit in hundreds of thousands of dollars or more before they are allowed to bid at the sales.

Over-the-counter sales are where the tax collector sells the tax liens or tax deeds to the open public on a first come first serve basis after the open public sale. This is when the tax collector has several parcels in their inventory that they now want to sell. They are not required to advertise the availability of these properties; all you have to do is go to the tax collector and ask for the list of available properties and then pay for the property. There is no competitive bidding for these properties, but you may want to ask yourself why these properties were not sold at the sale. Before you obligate yourself to buy any of these properties, you need to do your due diligence first.

Lottery sales are done in some states such as they recently did in Clark County, Nevada. The bidders are preregistered, and everyone is given a bidder number. Numbers are randomly drawn out for each parcel they are selling a tax lien on, and if your number is called, you either take the tax lien or pass. They will sometimes call a second position on the tax lien in case the first does not pay up within twenty-four hours of the tax sale. This is another great way to purchase tax liens in an area where property values are very high as the interest rate cannot be bid down and everyone gets a deal. Better yet is if the owner does not pay off the tax lien in the fixed amount of time you will get the deed to the property. I recently had two of my students from my tax lien seminar attend the Clark County, Nevada, tax lien sale and purchased two tax liens for around $8,000 for which the two properties have a value of over $700,000. Now that's a great deal, and as I always say, "You need to be in the game to win."

Below is a list of those states where you can buy the tax liens or tax deeds over the counter from the tax collector or by mailed in bid. Remember that when a property is sold at a tax deed sale, there are no interest rates listed because you get the property and the owner does not get the property back.

Alabama: Tax lien sale, 12% interest
Arkansas: Tax deed sales
Arizona: Tax lien sales, 16% interest
Florida: Tax lien, 18% interest + deed sales
Iowa: Tax lien sales, 24% interest
Kansas: Tax deed sales
Michigan: Tax deed sales
Minnesota: Tax deed sales
Montana: Tax lien sales, 10% interest
Nebraska: Tax lien sales, 14% interest
New Jersey: Tax lien sales, 18% interest
Oklahoma: Tax lien sales, 8% interest
South Carolina: Tax lien sales, 12% interest
South Dakota: Tax lien sales, 12% interest
Texas: Tax deed sales, 25% interest
Utah: Tax deed sale

CHAPTER 2

Due Diligence Made Easy

Researching Properties Before You Bid

Before you bid on any property at a tax sale, you need to do some research which I call due diligence.

I have the following forms that I like to use when evaluating properties, and they are used when I prepare to go to a sale.

File #________
Property research checklist
Property evaluation sheet_____
P.A.C.E.R. (Public access to court electronic records)_____
Tax collector online data_____
Property appraiser's tax map_____
Property appraiser's plat map_____
MapQuest address search_____
Drive by property, use worksheet_____
County clerk records search by name_____
Public utility lien search_____
Call local realtor for comps_____
Maximum bid established_____

Your file number__________

Property evaluation sheet

1. Date of the tax sale
2. Tax lien certificate or tax deed number:
3. Location of the property: Nearest cross street:
4. Legal description/property identification number:
5. Property dimensions/square footage: House square footage:
6. Property use or zoning:
7. Current listed owner's name and address:
8. Assessed values: Land = $__________________ Buildings = $__________________ Other structure = $__________________ Total = $__________________
9. Area comps: Land = $__________________ Improvements = $__________________ Other structure = $__________________ Total = $__________________
10. My minimum bid: $__________ My maximum bid: $__________ Sale date:________________
11. *Do not exceed* amount I am willing to bid up to:

Municipality:________________ Date of sale: __________
County: ___________ State: _____Today's date: _________

Property ID # Photo 1 Photo 2 Photo 3 Photo 4 Area Condition Building Confidence
__________ □□ □□ □□ □□ 1 2 3 4 5 1 2 3 4 5 1 2 3 4 5

SF 2-4 4+ Cnd Twnh Off C Cnd Htl Wh Rtl Mx Rel Ind MH Vres Vcom Vind Agr Plot Pgar
□ □ □ □ □ □ □ □ □ □ □ □ □ □ □ □ □ □ □ □
BU BO UN AB EPA FS NF Additional Comments # of Bd Ups
□ □ □ □ □ □ □

Property ID # Photo 1 Photo 2 Photo 3 Photo 4 Area Condition Building Confidence
__________ □□ □□ □□ □□ 1 2 3 4 5 1 2 3 4 5 1 2 3 4 5

SF 2-4 4+ Cnd Twnh Off C Cnd Htl Wh Rtl Mx Rel Ind MH Vres Vcom Vind Agr Plot Pgar
□ □ □ □ □ □ □ □ □ □ □ □ □ □ □ □ □ □ □ □
BU BO UN AB EPA FS NF Additional Comments # of Bd Ups
□ □ □ □ □ □ □

Property ID # Photo 1 Photo 2 Photo 3 Photo 4 Area Condition Building Confidence
__________ □□ □□ □□ □□ 1 2 3 4 5 1 2 3 4 5 1 2 3 4 5

SF 2-4 4+ Cnd Twnh Off C Cnd Htl Wh Rtl Mx Rel Ind MH Vres Vcom Vind Agr Plot Pgar
□ □ □ □ □ □ □ □ □ □ □ □ □ □ □ □ □ □ □ □
BU BO UN AB EPA FS NF Additional Comments # of Bd Ups
□ □ □ □ □ □ □

Property ID # Photo 1 Photo 2 Photo 3 Photo 4 Area Condition Building Confidence
__________ □□ □□ □□ □□ 1 2 3 4 5 1 2 3 4 5 1 2 3 4 5

SF 2-4 4+ Cnd Twnh Off C Cnd Htl Wh Rtl Mx Rel Ind MH Vres Vcom Vind Agr Plot Pgar
□ □ □ □ □ □ □ □ □ □ □ □ □ □ □ □ □ □ □ □
BU BO UN AB EPA FS NF Additional Comments # of Bd Ups
□ □ □ □ □ □ □

When you are driving an area where a property is located, you need to keep track of your research and be able to segment your market. You need to use the forms provided to keep a record of the information you have acquired from visually inspecting the properties. Once all of your research has been completed, you are now ready to attend the sale.

How To Be a Smart Bidder

It is best to know the type of bidding method used at the sale prior to you arriving on the date of the actual tax sale. You should go visit the tax collector a few weeks before the sale and ask them if they could sit down with you and have them explain the tax sale process in their specific area and how the bidding works. It has been my experience that they are more than willing to spend some time with you to explain how it works now as opposed to dealing with you after the sale because you want to back out of the lien you just purchased at the sale.

At the tax lien sale, it is best to sit a few rows back from the front. The reason is that the regulars (or big players as I like to call them) like to sit there, and this way, you can keep an eye on them and see what they are doing. When you are ready to start bidding on properties, you need to create your own bid sheet which will have your limits already established. You will have this bid sheet out in front of you to keep you from getting caught up in the bidding frenzy and paying too much.

For example, if there is a property at a tax lien sale and the tax lien amount is $800, and the maximum interest rate is 18%, you may be willing to go as low as 15%. You need to be careful not to be drawn into a bidding war and get the lien for an amount much lower then you had desired. When you are at the tax deed sale, you need to know the highest amount that you are willing to bid on the property over the tax lien amount ahead of time. This is determined by getting the actual value of the property based on its current condition and deciding what percent of the actual value you would be willing to pay (sample bid sheet: index 1). You also want to keep in mind that if you get the property, what you are going to do with it or your exit strategy will be. Your options may be to sell it fast by getting a small profit or to fix it up and sell it to a homeowner or an investor.

You also need to determine what your ROI (return on investment) will be for both strategies.

How to Determine the ROI

Most all seasoned investors as well as beginners use the "return on investment" (commonly referred to as ROI) as a way to determine if a property is a good deal or not. The way you determine the ROI is that you take the profit and divide it by the amount you invested, and that will give you a return on investment (ROI). This can be used for almost any property and can also be used for rental property based on the annual income and the amount initially invested. Let's see how it actually works with tax deeds.

For example, you bid on a property (it needs a lot of work) that in its current condition is worth $30,000, and you get it for a bid of $22,000. You then list the property low and sell it quickly for $26,000 to another investor. To determine the ROI, you take the $4,000 profit ($26,000 sale price less the $22,000 purchase price) and then divide by $22,000 cost (your purchase price) to determine your return on your investment is 18%. If you decide to fix it up and then sell it for a profit that you need to add the fix up cost. You would then calculate the fix up cost to be $29,000, but the property now has an after repaired value of $75,000. The total amount you now have invested is increased to $51,000, and if you want to sell it quickly, you can now sell it for $70,000 and you have the following ROI. You take the profit of $19,000 ($70,000 less the $51,000) and divide it by $70 to get a ROI of 27%.

Different Maturity Dates

With tax lien certificates, you only have a lien on the property and do not actually have an ownership interest in the property. Since we have a lien on the property, it is as if we are making a loan to the tax collector on behalf of the property owner. Since you are loaning the money to the tax collector for the homeowner, the loan will have a maturity date which is commonly referred to as the redemption date. This redemption date varies from state to state and can be anywhere from one year to three years.

During this period, you are waiting for your tax lien certificate to mature during which you will be entitled to a fixed interest rate of return on the amount of the tax lien certificate. When your tax lien certificate matures, you now have the ability to start the tax lien foreclosure and apply for a tax deed.

The states that have tax deed sales also may have a maturity date in which you must hold the property while the redemption period runs out. Although there are not a lot of states that have tax deed sales with a redemption period, they will offer the purchaser an interest rate in the form of a penalty for the owner to get there property back. Texas, for example, is a tax deed state with a 25% penalty during the first six months after you buy the property at the tax sale on nonowner occupied or nonagricultural properties.

Procedure for Starting the Tax Foreclosure

This is the process when you purchase a tax lien certificate and you now want to get the deed to the property. You must wait the one to three years of the redemption period to lapse, and this is where the owner has the opportunity to get their property back by paying the full amount of the taxes plus all of the interest and fees to the holder of the tax lien certificate. Now that the redemption time is over, you now can apply to have your tax lien certificate turned into a tax deed, and this process will vary from state to state. Most of the states require you to do a judicial foreclosure action in the courts to clear the title, and you get issued a final judgment from the state court. This is a basic foreclosure action and can be completed by an individual if the tax lien was purchased by that individual, although it is recommended that this be done by an attorney who specializes in this area of the law.

In all cases, I always recommend that the tax lien foreclosure be done by an attorney who specializes in that field of law because you have so much at stake, and it's your money. There are a few other states that only require that you apply for a tax deed and you exchange your tax lien for a tax deed. In these cases, you hold your tax lien certificate for the prescribed amount of time, and after that time has lapsed, you turn your tax lien certificate into the tax collector, and they in turn give you a tax deed.

There are also some states that will actually do the foreclosure for you. This is where the county clerk processes the tax lien foreclosure for a small fee. In these cases, the property is again offered for sale by open bidding, and if no one bids on that specific property where you held the tax lien, then you are given a tax deed. Each of the specific state rules and procedures will be covered later in this book.

Paperwork Used for a Typical Tax Lien Foreclosure

The states again will vary on what documents need to be used in a foreclosure action, but we will try to give you the basic forms used.

Usually, the first document sent out is a notice to the property owner and others who hold an interest in the property, and we call them the defendants. This letter is to advise the defendants that a foreclosure is about to start and that you are demanding payment in full by a certain date. In some states, this is referred to a "thirty-day letter." This is a letter sent out via regular and certified mail to all the defendants indicating the location of the property and the amount to redeem the lien on the property.

The next document is a complaint and summons that is sent out to all the owners and creditors that have an interest in the property. The complaint is the legal document served on all of the defendants that explain who, what, where, and why there is a legal action against the defendants. It is usually a few pages long, and once served on the defendants, they have a fixed period of time to send in a written answer which is usually within thirty-five days from the date they were served.

The default is the next document used when the defendants fail to file an answer after they were served the summons and the complaint.

At this point, the defendants are given another chance to pay off the lien, and this is sometimes referred to as the OST which stands for "order setting the time, place, and amount of redemption." This will specify the amount to pay off the tax lien, the last day that they can pay off this lien, and the location of the tax collector's office.

The last document is the final judgment where a judge of the state court has declared that you completed the foreclosure in compliance with the state statutes and issues this document that transfers the rights of ownership from the owner of the property to us the investor.

Purchase a tax sale certificate	January 1, 2000
Get tax sale certificate recorded	January 1, 2000
Pay taxes over the next two years	January 1, 2002
Certificate matures; start foreclosure	January 1, 2002
File a notice of lis pendens	January 1, 2002
Order a title search	January 1, 2002
Send out a "thirty-day notice"	February 1, 2002
Complaint filed	March 1, 2002
Summons and complaint served	April 1, 2002
Default filed on all defendants	June 1, 2002
OST requested from the courts	July 1, 2002
Request final judgment from the court	August 1, 2002
Final judgment signed by the court	September 1, 2002
Send final judgment to be recorded	September 1, 2002
Warrant of removal served on property	October 1, 2002
Sell or keep the property	thirty-four months' time

See enclosed foreclosure forms in Appendix
Sample time frame from start to finish:
New Jersey tax lien process

CHAPTER 3

Seven Myths of Tax Lien Investing

In 1998, my wife and I needed a way to earn extra money. While at work, I learned a little about tax liens that were sold by tax collectors to investors for very little money. Since we had very little and needed extra money for our family, I did some research and, to my disappointment, could not find much at all on the subject. The *myths: the truth* is what we faced before we attained the success we have today. Had I yielded to those myths, I would still be working a nine to five *job*.

In this book, I will walk you through all the doubts and fears we were faced with every day while we started on this venture. Although we knew we could make it, many around us had their doubts and fears, while a few supported us. We had a few very good friends and family to encourage us, and for that, we are sincerely grateful.

Since you are already reading this book, I know you have decided to make a difference in your life. I know that once you believe you can do it and the only fear is fear itself, you will be ready for the next step. We offer many support packages, and if you go to our website, www.TaxLienAndDeed.com, you will see that we have many educational tools ready to be put into place immediately. We have all types of trainings going on at different locations across the country and hope that you have the opportunity to meet me at one of these so I can shake your hand and congratulate you on this journey.

My hope is that you will study all of special concepts and strategies and implement them to start your success. As you start putting into practice all the techniques and secrets to investing you have acquired, you should start to benefit as you see the results. You then have the ability to help your family and friends with this knowledge.

Thomas J. Senatore
President, TLD International, LLC

Myth 1: I Can Only Invest Where I Live

I have been involved with investing for many years now, and this is something I have always heard. It is not true, and I am not sure where or how it started. I can tell you this: I have purchased properties across the United States and in many cases have never even seen the property.

Let me start from the beginning.

As a beginner investor, I was taught to buy in an area within thirty-sixty minutes of where I lived. Since I was new at this, I thought it made sense and did all of my investing in the different counties around where I lived. In the beginning, it worked well, but then I found there were deals to be made and they might not be close. I had to choose to either go out on a limb or try something that had not been encouraged. If I stayed close to home, I would do well but would not grow and develop my strategy, so I ventured off against the myths.

The first time I went out of my area was when I went to Trenton, New Jersey, to look at a few properties. It was probably about 90–120 minutes away depending on the time of the day. Now, for many, this alone would stop you immediately, but not me. I did this trip many times, and as I continued, I found I was learning more and more of the area. After some time, I was as comfortable here as I was in my own town. Now, let me say this right away. I am not encouraging you to drive hours and hours every day. What I am saying is that you need to expand your horizon a little more.

The first deal I did was a single-family house that was attached to another house in an average area. This is referred to as a *twin*-style constructed home. There were nice homes all around, some needed a bit of work, and others had been remodeled. I felt comfortable working in this area and took on the project. But here is the catch to this entire example. First, it was not a tax lien I purchased, it was another investor's. Second, we used his money to enhance the property, not a penny of my money was used. Third, I got 50% of the profits because I ran the project from start to finish and any work I did I was paid for by the investor. So with that being said, let's take a look at the project.

Here is the property when I got there. The investor had purchased the tax lien by way of an assignment from another investor. What that means is it was sold at the tax lien sale to one investor, and then that investor sold it to another investor. The second investor is the one I was working with, and he took the tax lien into the foreclosure process and was able to secure the tax deed by way of a final judgment from the courts. With this final judgment, the title was transferred, and I was now able to go to the property for this investor and see what we are working with.

Why did the investor pick me? First, he knew I was active with buying tax liens, and second, he knew I had a background in construction.

If we look over the picture on the previous page, we see that this home is in need of some work. The property is a three-story home with a garage to the left of the home and is attached to an enclosed porch. What I need to do is look at the aerial photo of the area to see what the other homes are like on North Eastfield Avenue.

Here is an aerial view of the neighborhood.

The house we have is the second in from the corner on the right side of the street. It is close to a park, and there are nice homes on both sides of the street. The remodel only took a few months and none of my money. The investor paid for all the cost of the work, and then I was able to enjoy 50% of the profits. The property ended up being a very nice home and was sold in no time at all.

Let see what the finished product looked like.

When the deal closed, and all the funds were paid out, it will be like this.

Tax lien costs $23,000, and the rehab was another $35,000 which meant there was $58,000 into the deal. The property was sold for $135,000, and after closing costs, the amount left over was close to $70,000 which meant we each got around $35,000 each. That ends up being a return of 60% for the investor and infinity for me since I had nothing in the deal in the first place. I like this example for two reasons: one, it can be done away from home, and two, it can be done without money.

Myth 2: Can I Really Make 18% or Better

When I speak to investors around the country and overseas, I often get asked this question: is it realistic to believe I can get 18% on my money with the way the economy is going?

My answer to them would be they can't if they think they cannot, but if they think they can, it is all possible. I have been getting 18% on my tax liens for some time and on my tax deeds even better. On the last deal I just did, I was able to make 17% on the deal. Well, backup. I thought I just said I get 18% or better on my deals. Well, what I did not tell you was that the 17% return was based on the profit from the deal, but I only had the property for five days.

That would be about 107% for the month, or better yet, it would be 1224% for the year.

When we buy the tax liens, I place bids at the 18% mark, and if I get the lien, it's great, and if I do not, then I wait till the next one comes about. I typically get close to 30% of all my bids accepted at 18% which is very good percentages.

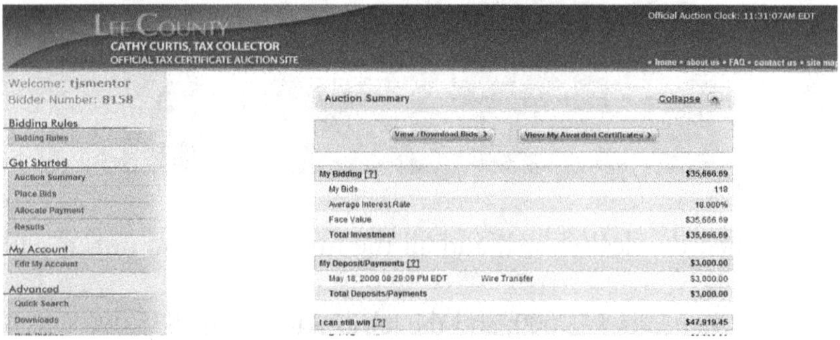

LEE COUNTY
CATHY CURTIS, TAX COLLECTOR
OFFICIAL TAX CERTIFICATE AUCTION SITE
Official Auction Clock: 11:31:07AM EDT
• home • about us • FAQ • contact us • site map

Welcome: tjsmentor
Bidder Number: 8158

Bidding Rules: Bidding Rules
Get Started: Auction Summary · Place Bids · Allocate Payment · Results
My Account: Edit My Account
Advanced: Quick Search · Downloads

Auction Summary — Collapse

View / Download Bids › View My Awarded Certificates ›

My Bidding [?]		**$35,666.69**
My Bids		118
Average Interest Rate		18.000%
Face Value		$35,666.69
Total Investment		**$35,666.69**
My Deposit/Payments [?]		**$3,000.00**
May 18, 2009 08:29:09 PM EDT	Wire Transfer	$3,000.00
Total Deposits/Payments		**$3,000.00**
I can still win [?]		**$47,919.45**

As you can see, I bid 18% on all the tax liens, and when the auction was completed, I had won forty-six tax liens that day all at 18% with a face value of $12,080.55. The price of the liens I won was between $180 and $2,500 which is a price I am sure everyone can afford. I know that if I can do this over the Internet, it does not matter if I have ten years' experience or ten days experience. The great thing about the Internet auctions is that the computer does not know the background of the bidders.

Here is the summary of the auction from my second account.

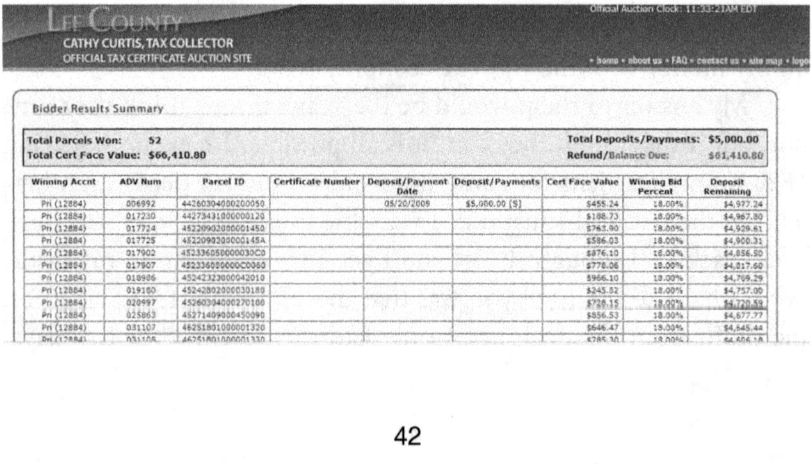

LEE COUNTY
CATHY CURTIS, TAX COLLECTOR
OFFICIAL TAX CERTIFICATE AUCTION SITE
Official Auction Clock: 11:33:21AM EDT
• home • about us • FAQ • contact us • site map • logout

Bidder Results Summary

Total Parcels Won:	**52**	**Total Deposits/Payments:**	**$5,000.00**
Total Cert Face Value:	**$66,410.80**	**Refund/Balance Due:**	**$61,410.80**

Winning Accnt	ADV Num	Parcel ID	Certificate Number	Deposit/Payment Date	Deposit/Payments	Cert Face Value	Winning Bid Percent	Deposit Remaining
Pri (12884)	006992	44260304000200050		05/20/2009	$5,000.00 (S)	$455.24	18.00%	$4,977.24
Pri (12884)	017230	44273431000000120				$188.73	18.00%	$4,967.80
Pri (12884)	017724	45220902000001450				$763.90	18.00%	$4,929.61
Pri (12884)	017725	4522090200000145A				$586.03	18.00%	$4,900.31
Pri (12884)	017902	45233605000030C0				$876.10	18.00%	$4,856.50
Pri (12884)	017907	4523360500000C0060				$778.06	18.00%	$4,817.60
Pri (12884)	018986	45242323000042010				$966.10	18.00%	$4,769.29
Pri (12884)	019160	45242802000030180				$245.82	18.00%	$4,757.00
Pri (12884)	020997	45260304000270100				$728.15	18.00%	$4,720.59
Pri (12884)	025863	45271409000450090				$856.53	18.00%	$4,677.77
Pri (12884)	031107	46251801000001320				$646.47	18.00%	$4,645.44
Pri (12884)	031108	46251801000001330				$785.30	18.00%	$4,606.18

With this account, I was able to purchase fifty-two tax liens, and the face value was at $66,410. That would mean that the average tax lien face value was around $1,200 which is affordable as well.

Now you may ask why other investors are not doing this if it is so profitable. The reason is that they most likely do not know about this system. Many people have seen this strategy advertised either on TV or at a seminar that they attended. The problem is that they try too hard to sell the strategy, and they often only give the unique deal or the extreme profit potential. For example, I bought this home for $80 and sold it for $250,000. While that may be true, there most certainly is a bit of information that is missing. One may be that it was purchased for $80, but the picture you see is after they put $180,000 into the property and sold it two years later. While that is truly a great deal in and on itself, the information may be misdirecting, and that is why most people stay away from the tax liens and the tax deeds. I like to show the very ugly houses I buy for $2,000 and sell a day or two later for $6,000. Or the tax lien I had under contract to buy and sold to another investor the same day for a profit of over $4,000. These are the nuts and bolts of our business, and if you invest wisely and build a system like the one I am teaching you, the profits will come.

I have for years done better than 18% per year combined on the tax liens and the tax deeds. If I were to say a number, I would have to guess that I make about 8%–10% per month in profits. If you were to try to do the same, all you would need to do is be active and buy on a regular basis. If you look at all the tax liens I have purchased over the last five years, you would see that my cumulative interest earned was in the area of 16%–17%. If you add the tax deeds that I have purchased over the same time, the interest earned would be at least 2% per month, sometimes even higher. I have had properties that I have purchased from taxes, remodeled and then sold retail that have earned well over 1000% for the year. The results are based on the effort; you put in a lot of effort, and you will see results that are proportionate.

Myth 3: Only Swamp Land Is Available

If you were to look at the sales, whether they are tax liens or tax deeds, they cover all types of properties. I myself like to look at raw land that is situated in desirable neighborhoods. These would be the vacant lots that are near other improved lots in areas that have been well developed. I like to search all the properties to see if I can find the corner lot which are more desirable.

Here is a sample of six of fifty-seven properties listed at the next auction.

What I have done is copy the images on the list to view.

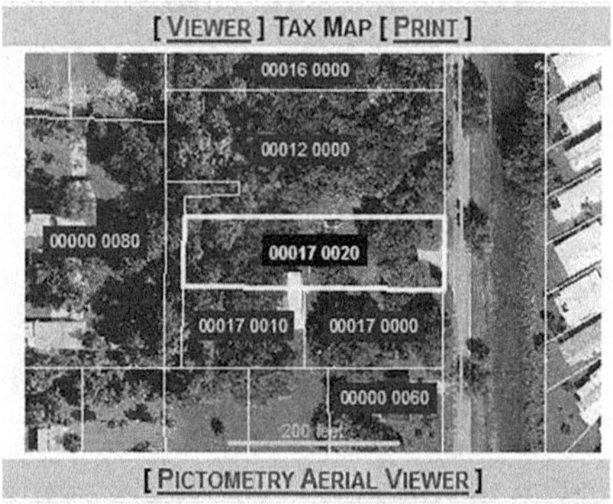

Tax deed # 009, open taxes of $1559.73

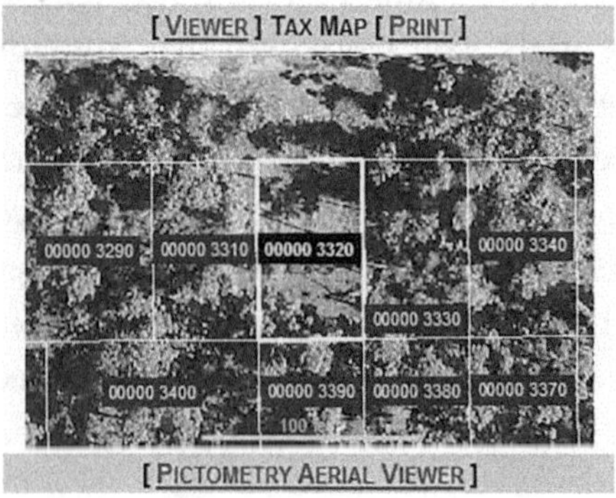

Tax deed # 010, open taxes of $1914.93

As you can see from the first two photos, these are vacant lots in residential areas and would have a resale value of approximately $4,500 each. If I were to purchase these, I could resell them for $3,000 each and net almost $1,000 per lot.

The next two properties:

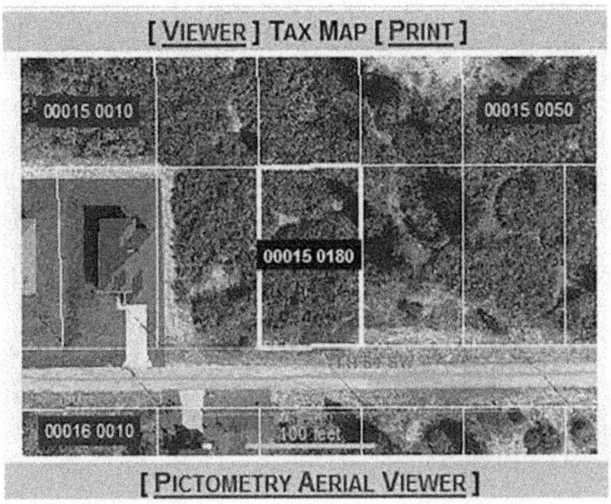

Tax deed #010, open taxes of $2,057.22

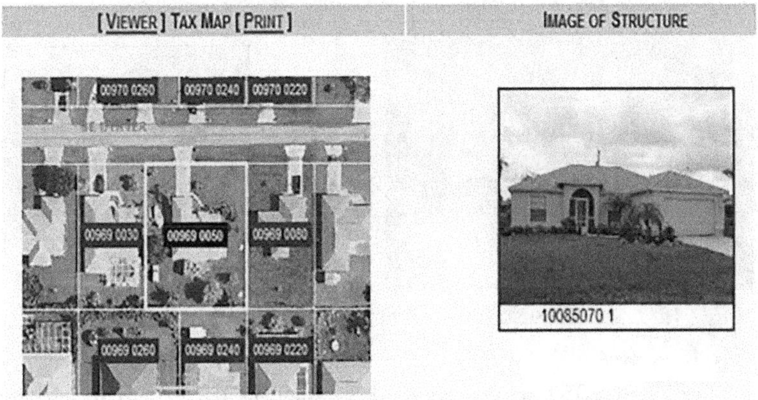

Tax deed # 047, open taxes of $13,115.99 for a house that has a market value of over $150,000 and could easily be sold for over $120,000.

This is one of the better properties although this is not the best one on that list. There is a property listed as an open bid of $167,827.39 with a market value of $3,176,820,000 that is located in Boca Grande, Florida. Now that is a property to watch and buy.

The last set of the first six properties is as shown below.

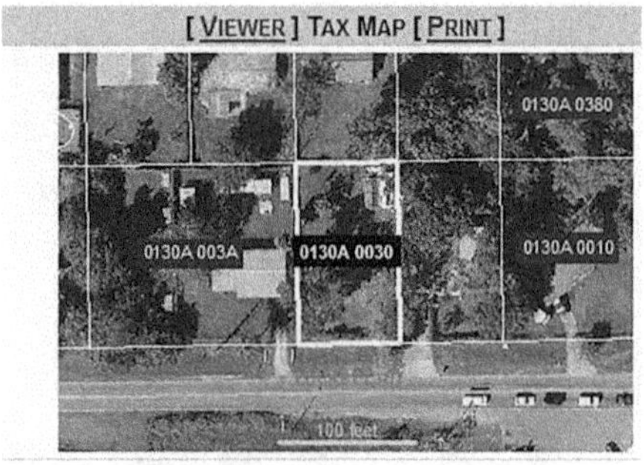

Tax deed #049, open taxes of $2,362.22 for a vacant residential lot that may have had a structure on it at one time.

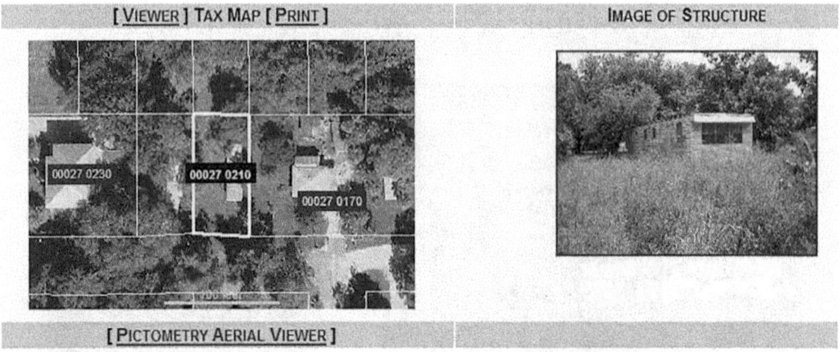

Tax deed #051, open taxes of $1,849.52 for an improved residential lot that currently has a mobile home situated on the property.

If I were to get this property, the mobile home transfers with the deed in most all cases and I now have an income generating property for possibly $2,000.

Myth 4: The Banks Will Buy the Property First?

With the way the economy goes in cycles, the banks cannot keep track of all the properties that end up being sold for the back taxes. Each year, several hundred to several hundred thousand homes are lost in foreclosure either for nonpayment of taxes or the nonpayment of the mortgage.

With every real estate boom, there is a real estate crash, and no matter what the times are, there will always be a way to make large amounts of profits here. Tax liens and tax deeds seem to not be affected by the economy and the events that happen all around. The banks on the other hand are directly affected. Let's look at it this way. When the banks are doing extremely well, they are not concerned about the few homes that may be lost for taxes as they will pursue the property owners, and these properties fall through the cracks. When times are bad, the mortgage company needs to keep every spare person and hour attempting to collect the funds needed to stay afloat, and they often have property fall by the way side.

So what is the story with the banks? The banks are in the business of lending and holding our money; they are not in the business of holding real estate. Banks issue mortgages for properties, and the owners sign a promissory note for the amount. The bank then at times attempts to sell off the debt to another bank or investor. Over time, the note and mortgage documents are lost and possibly the payments as well. The original bank may be getting the funds, but the note is held by someone else. This is where all the fun starts. The first bank gets notice of the delinquency, and they have been getting paid by the homeowner. They respond back by saying they do not hold the mortgage or note on the property, and they do not try to find out who does as they have no financial incentive to do so. Now these notices get sent to the lien holders as well as the property owners, and the failure by any party to do something to stop this will result in the loss of the deed to the tax lien investor.

I can't tell you how many times I have gone to an auction of property for back taxes where the property owner is the bank as they have taken the property back in foreclosure, and yet they too have failed to pay the property taxes. This occurrence happens every day, and it does not matter if the economy is good or the economy is bad, banks have too much going on, and we, as investors, can gain so much here.

On our website (www.TaxLienAndDeed.com), we have the lists of all the sales that happen around the country, and we offer a huge discount for the enhanced list where the owner of the property is listed, and for many of the properties, the owner is a *bank*!

Some of you may be confused as you have seen Wachovia Bank or Bank of America as the listed lien holder or they are listed as the bidder at the tax deed sale. Actually, what you are seeing is that these two banks fund the investors who buy on a regular basis and that the money is what they refer to as "collateralized." Here is an example of the title if I were to borrow the money from the bank to buy properties. The owner would be listed as Wachovia Bank collateral agent for *Tax Lien and Deed.com* so that all property I buy, the bank would be the first one paid when the property is sold.

What happens with a private mortgage and the bank is an individual? With the two homes listed for tax deed sale, each of the parcels has a mortgage, and the mortgagor is an individual. On the next page, we have copied the mortgage information for your review.

Parcel ID #: 25-44-23-C2-00969.0050
Grantee(s) SS#:

MTG DOC 658.35
INTANGIBLE 376.28
DEPUTY CLERK L Ambrosio

(3)

MORTGAGE DEED

This MORTGAGE DEED executed on **July 27, 2005**, by **JONATHAN JOSHUA THORN, a single person, PAUL JASON ECKENRODE, a single person, and BRETT MICHAEL ECKENRODE, a single person,** whose post office address is **612 SE 17th Ter., Cape Coral, FL 33990**, hereinafter called the MORTGAGOR, to **WILHELMINIA M. MOUNT**, whose post office address is **4541 Randag Drive, North Fort Myers, FL 33917**, hereinafter called the MORTGAGEE:

(Wherever used herein the terms "MORTGAGOR" and "MORTGAGEE" include all the parties to this instrument and the heirs, legal representatives and assigns of individuals, and the successors and assigns of corporations; and the term "NOTE" includes all the notes herein described if more than one.)

WITNESSETH, that for good and valuable considerations and also in consideration of the aggregate sum named in the promissory note of even date herewith, hereinafter described, the MORTGAGOR hereby grants, bargains, sells, aliens, remises, conveys and confirms unto the mortgagee all the certain

Notice that in both of the mortgage deeds, the mortgagor is a person and not a bank. Both of these individuals will lose their collateral if they do not redeem this from the auction. At that time, they will need to chase the owner for the money.

Parcel ID #: 25-44-23-C2-00969.0050
Grantee(s) SS#:

MTG DOC 658.35
INTANGIBLE 376.28
DEPUTY CLERK L Ambrosio

(3)

MORTGAGE DEED

This MORTGAGE DEED executed on **July 27, 2005**, by **JONATHAN JOSHUA THORN, a single person, PAUL JASON ECKENRODE, a single person, and BRETT MICHAEL ECKENRODE, a single person**, whose post office address is **612 SE 17th Ter., Cape Coral, FL 33990**, hereinafter called the MORTGAGOR, to **WILHELMINIA M. MOUNT**, whose post office address is **4541 Randag Drive, North Fort Myers, FL 33917**, hereinafter called the MORTGAGEE:

(Wherever used herein the terms "MORTGAGOR" and "MORTGAGEE" include all the parties to this instrument and the heirs, legal representatives and assigns of individuals, and the successors and assigns of corporations; and the term "NOTE" includes all the notes herein described if more than one.)

WITNESSETH, that for good and valuable considerations and also in consideration of the aggregate sum named in the promissory note of even date herewith, hereinafter described, the MORTGAGOR hereby grants, bargains, sells, aliens, remises, conveys and confirms unto the mortgagee all the certain

Myth 5: If I Win, I Have to Pay the Mortgage?

In many instances, the properties you buy at the tax sale have no debts with the exception of the property taxes. These are relatively easy to explain since the owners have forgotten about the property, given up on the property, or have passed away with the heirs not wanting the property. I have seen homes where the parents have passed on, and they left the house to the four surviving children. The home is in need of some cosmetic repairs, and taxes and insurance need to be paid. The problem is one or more of the siblings refuse to pay, and that leads to all not paying. In the end, the property gets sold for back taxes which could be as low as $3000, and the property had a market value of $100,000.

Now comes the same home, but let us add a mortgage of $150,000 on the property, and the market value is still at $100,000. The taxes on this property are at $3,000 per year, but the bank cannot afford to keep funding the property as they already funded the insurance. The bank's desire is to get the mortgage foreclosure completed before the tax lien is completed.

There is what we call priority of liens when it comes to the tax sales. The highest priority in any situation wins, and in our case, it is the taxes. With property taxes, the lien is a government lien and must be paid. Out of most all of the government liens out there, I believe a property tax lien is the most difficult to reduce or eliminate. With that said, if I have a home I am looking at, it is most likely to have several types of liens against it.

The liens that are directly on the property have more priority power than those that are attached from the owner's actions or failure thereof. If an owner has work done on the house and fails to pay, then a mechanics lien is attached to the property. If the owner has work completed at his office and does not pay, the person will attach a mechanics lien against the individual and all property he owns including the house. The first mechanics lien would have priority over the second. If there was a mortgage on that property, it would have priority over both. Should there be a second mortgage on that property, it would be subordinate to the first mortgage but superior to the mechanics liens. Now the fun begins as a tax lien no matter what is superior to the mortgage lien and must be paid if the mortgage company takes ownership. A mortgage cannot eliminate government lien.

If we have a government lien foreclosing, then all the other debts fall off the title, but they still remain on the individual. What happens when we have several governmental liens on the same property, which one has priority, and which ones fall by the side? We all know that the IRS is the highest type of lien there is, and yet it is not as powerful as a tax lien. In many instances, the IRS will yield their position to the tax lien if the tax lien is foreclosing for nonpayment of the property taxes. The mortgage is wiped off the property, but the IRS is offered a 180-day window to redeem the property tax lien or lift their lien from the property. This does not come up that often, and when it does, you should have your attorney look into the matter quickly.

But for the purposes of this chapter, here is all you need to know. When I buy a tax lien property, I am essentially getting the property free and clear of all liens that were placed upon the property prior to the foreclosure action commencing. In English, if a lien was placed yesterday, then it passes on to you; if it were placed last year before the action started, then it is wiped off the title.

Myth 6: I Only Have a Small Amount of Money?

How much one needs is not an issue for you to worry about. What you need to ask yourself is how much you want to make. I started this business with only a $1,000 and over five years turned it into over a million dollars. I would love to say that I did it with very little effort and that my system then was automated, and all I did was check my computer every day to see how much money I was making, but that would not be true. What I did was to work the system I created every day till it was refined to the tax lien buying system we offer today. I spent about fifteen hours every week on tax lien buying and researching to make to process as simplified as possible. When we started, there was nothing out there for us to compare to, so we used the trial and error method and made it work.

We show an example in my live trainings where I turned $1,000 into almost a million dollars. During my presentation, I explain that it was not overnight; in fact, it took almost ten years to complete. We had to find the balance due for the lien of $24,000 in five weeks, of which we did. I then had to find a way to cover the $80,000 in repair cost over the next eight months while I fixed up the building, of which we did. Then I had to rent out the property for cash flow over the next four years till the market improved and was able to sell at a great price, of which we did. To complete the deal, we offered owner financing on the deal and have been receiving monthly payments of $2,666.67 for over three years and have just about sixteen more payments to go. Oh, the best part is that when the payments are finished, the balance due is $440,000 which is not too bad. But like I said, it all started with my check for $1,000 and about ten years of time, but in the end, we pocketed over $800,000.

How do you start out if you have only, say, $5,000 and a little free time to invest? As I train classes and provide mentor trainings, I get this all the time. Why not pick up a tax lien at 18% for about $800 and then look for a tax deed for say $4,000? If you can turn the tax deed for a 25% return, you would receive a check for $5,000, and the $800 would still be growing. If you turn around and invest the $5,000 and get paid $7,000 and do this over the course of a year, you would end up with at least $58,207.66. That is assuming you were able to buy and sell within thirty days or less. This return would be a tenfold profit of what you started with. If you were to follow the same system, the next year you would have more money than you could ever imagine. What we are doing is using compounding interest to our benefit, and in twenty-four months after we invested the first $5,000, we could potentially have $847,000.

Now I can hear everyone now saying that it cannot be done. So let's imagine for one minute it is possible, but you can only achieve 50% of what I say, then you would have only $423,000 instead. I like to have investors think big and hope for the stars. Now that we have the goals I like to attain, I will show you what the low side of the goals would be like. For this, I will chart out a scenario that everyone could accomplish.

What I have below is the strategy I have implemented and currently working on to use when I have my live trainings. These figures are realistic and accurate.

Start with only $5,000.

Month number one
Buy a tax deed on a property valued at $15 for no more than $4,000.
List the property on eBay and craigslist for $7,000; sell for $6,000.
Profit is $2,000.

Month number two
Start the month with $7,000 in the bank.
Buy two tax deeds for properties valued at $15 for no more than $3,500.

List the property on eBay and craigslist for $7,000; sell for $6,000.
Profit is $2,500 each, or $5,000 total.

Month number three
Start the month with $12,000 in the bank.
Buy three tax deeds for properties valued at $15 for no more than $3,500.
List the property on eBay and craigslist for $7,000; sell for $6,000.
Profit is $2,500 each, or $7,500 total.

Month number four
Start the month with $19,500 in the bank.
Buy five tax deeds for properties valued at $15 for no more than $3,500.
List the property on eBay and craigslist for $7,000; sell for $6,000.
Profit is $2,500 each, or $12,500 total.

Month number five
Start the month with $32,000 in the bank.
Buy one tax deed for properties valued at $90,000 for no more than $30,000.
List the property on eBay and craigslist for $70,000; sell for $60,000.
Profit is $30,000 total.

Month number six
Start the month with $62,000 in the bank.
Buy two tax deeds for properties valued at $90,000 for no more than $30,000.
List the property on eBay and craigslist for $70,000; sell for $60,000.
Profit is $30,000 each, or $60,000 total.

Month number seven
Start the month with $122,000 in the bank.
Buy four tax deeds for properties valued at $90,000 for no more than $30,000.

List the property on eBay and craigslist for $70,000; sell for $60,000.
Profit is $30,000 each, or $120,000 total.

Month number eight
Start the month with $242,000 in the bank.
Buy two tax deeds for properties valued at $180,000 for no more than $90,000.
List the property on eBay and craigslist for $160,000; sell for $140,000.
Profit is $50,000 each, or $100,000 total.

As you can see from my process, it is simple yet profitable. All the properties we get we like to market at a price that can sell quickly. In our booklet series you received is one titled *The Profit Process.* Read that booklet over and over till you understand the process and can easily sell the properties you buy in less than thirty days.

Myth 7: I Can't Do It; It's Only for Rich People?

This is not just a game for the rich, but they do like to play here. Many of the wealthiest people have invested in real estate, and they at one time or another have been involved with tax liens. It may be that they had one on them or they purchased one, but in most cases, they have some understanding on them.

Over the years, I have come across investors from all levels, whether they are the beginner or they are the advanced. The thing that I see in common with all people is that they may have heard of investing in tax liens and tax deeds but that they failed to get started. At the auctions, I have seen the corporate purchaser (also known as institutional buyers) where they send out individuals to buy tax liens or the tax deeds. They get the funding from the banks, and they collateralize the purchases. Over time, I have seen these institutional buyers fall to the wayside and are no longer in business. The funds are in abundance, and they also dry up. It is the individual investor that I like to watch. There are many wealthy people investing in tax liens and tax deeds, but it is the small investors that make up the majority of the sales.

Don't confuse the thought that only the rich can do this or only those with money can do this, because both are not true. Yes, it always makes it a lot easier when you have money, but it is not a prerequisite to have a lot of money to start. In the previous chapter, I explained how to get started with only $5,000 in hand and how over two years' time it could be worth so much more. Here, I want to show you how it is done when you have no money in hand that can be used to invest. Remember that it does not take a lot of money rather then it takes a lot of determination.

I will explain below how to get started with investing in tax liens and tax deeds without the use of money. That's correct, I said without the use of money. I have set up systems where I have been able to invest for others at many different levels and have made so much money while doing it. Let me explain how that is done.

Find an individual who would like to earn 10% per year on the money they have whether it be in the bank, money market, stocks, or IRA. We explain that we have a system where the investment is secure and the profits are guaranteed. We also have a second investment where there is a small amount of risk, but the profits are much higher. I ask them if they are happy with the returns they are getting now, and I ask them if they do not mind to inform me at what interest rate of return they are at now. You would not be surprised to know that most people are only earning 3%–5% on their money. At this point, the questions start to fly, and you need to be ready.

They will ask you who, what, where, how, and why. You will try to slow them down but always be in control. I start out this way:

I have been working with a financial investor who deals in paper trading. He specializes in what is called tax lien certificate earnings, and we have been working together for some time.

Have you heard of this before? No matter what they say, your response would be, this has been going on for over forty years now, and there has been very little published on the subject. Would you like me to give you the short version? They most always say yes which is good because you probably could not give the long version anyway.

What happens is the tax collector needs income to run the county (city in some states), and when the property taxes are not paid, they seek to get the funds from investors like myself. I will go in to the tax collector and buy this paper debt, and the tax collector will guarantee me a return of 18%. I then hold this paper for twenty-four months while earning 18% each year till it is paid or I get the deed to the property. This system is not very complicated, and my partner, Tommy, and I have bought many of these over the past years.

There is *no* risk as the tax lien certificate is backed by the property which usually has over 90% equity in the property. I know this may sound hard to believe, but I assure you, it goes on every day, and we have been doing very well at this for many years.

You want to get them to agree to accept 10% interest on the money they will give you and then invest it mostly in tax liens at 18%. Take part of the funds and invest in tax deeds. After the year is up, you should have doubled the money you started with and paid the individual their money plus placed a huge profit in your pockets. I have been doing this for some time now and worked with individuals on a regular basis. We typically will take 30% of all the profits, and the individual gets the 70%. I like to think big, and when I get a fund of $100,000 or more, the potential grows exponentially.

Take an investment of $100,000 at 18%; on a bad day, you earn $6,000. Take the $100,000 and invest in tax deeds and increase the amount tenfold, and now we are talking a serious fund. You create a million-dollar profit, and your fee is $300,000, which I am sure would be a great improvement to any income you may have.

I hope you take all that I have provided and start to use this knowledge today. Knowledge is meant to be applied and not stored away for a rainy day. It is like a garden you plant for food, tend to it, and work with it and you eat for a lifetime. Let the garden tend to itself, and you grow hungry.

CHAPTER 4

Obstacles and Delays

What happens when you purchase a tax lien or a tax deed with redemption, and the owner decided to fight the tax foreclosure in court? Just imagine if the owner filed an answer to the "summons and complaint" you had served on him during the foreclosure process where they claimed they paid the taxes or that they were not served properly.

You or your attorney will have to file a motion in the court to challenge their claim. This will cost you time where the foreclosure is delayed up to sixty days as well as the additional cost of the legal fees. What defense if any does the owners have as a valid defense to the tax lien foreclosure?

The answer to this question is very simple: *none*! The only defense to a tax lien foreclosure is that they have a receipt to show that the taxes were paid for the period of time where the tax lien certificate was issued. This also is a potential problem and could cause a delay in getting the ownership of the property.

Bankruptcy and Your Money

What if the owner decided they have nothing left to lose and files a bankruptcy petition? This bankruptcy will give the owner an automatic stay, and all legal proceedings against them must stop immediately. Now you have your money tied up in a property, and you cannot touch it or the owner. What happens if the owner drags out the bankruptcy for five years? Then you have to wait the five years to get your money out of the property, but that may not be as bad as it sounds. You may wonder if you can lose your money if the owner files for bankruptcy, but that will not happen since a tax lien is a secured lien. Typically, the bankruptcy trustee decides what interest rate you can receive and in most case will give you the entire amount that is owed. So during the time the owner takes to pay off the tax lien, you will still be earning interest on your money.

What if the owner does not make the required monthly payments as agreed in the bankruptcy? Then you can request the bankruptcy trustee to remove the property from the bankruptcy protection and move forward with the foreclosure.

What I like to do is find properties that are in the foreclosure process where the owner is in a bankruptcy and then try to purchase the lien from the current lien holder at a discount. If the holder wants their money now, they may be willing to give you a discount as long as you do not mind waiting.

One thing you need to do before you start tracking all these properties in bankruptcy is to make sure a "proof of claim" was filed by the lien holder which makes them a secured lien holder and guarantees that they will be paid if the money is deposited by the debtor.

What Are Subsequent Taxes?

A subsequent tax is the property taxes that are due after your initial tax lien is issued. So if you purchased a tax lien in 2000, then the taxes due for the years 2001–2005 would be considered a subsequent tax, and as the lien holder, you would be entitled to pay that tax ten days after the due date and be entitled to the full interest amount of that state.

There are some states that do not permit a lien holder to buy the subsequent taxes such as the state of Florida. In Florida, they have a tax lien sale once a year, and they also have tax deed sales every month. If you buy the Florida tax lien certificate, you do not have to buy the following (also called subsequent) years' taxes.

When the tax lien holder requests there be a tax deed sale, they must pay off all other tax lien holders no matter when they purchased the tax lien certificate as long as it was not issued more than seven years old as the tax lien certificates in Florida expire seven years from the date of sale if not foreclosed on. When you do get a subsequent tax lien, you typically get an affidavit of subsequent taxes issued by the taxing authority. See enclosed affidavit: Index 2.

What happens if you purchase a tax lien in 2002, and you do not pay the subsequent taxes over the next three years? You will still hold a priority lien on the property that you can foreclose on, but, now, someone else has a lien superior to yours. What that means is another investor can start their own foreclosure and possibly wipe out your tax lien, and you end up with a worthless piece of paper. This is why I tell everyone who invests in tax liens that they need to be on top of all their liens and that they need to be sure they never miss paying any of the subsequent tax payments.

What Happens When the Deed Is Issued?

Once you obtain a tax deed, either by forcing the foreclosure or buying the property at a tax deed sale, the end results are similar. When you get the deed by foreclosing on a tax lien, the process is lengthy and can take as long as eighteen months. This is accomplished by obtaining a final judgment from the court that becomes the deed, and you now have full ownership to the property. Once you obtain ownership to the property, you first must get the property insured. It is at this point when you get the deed that you now have the right to go onto the property. Since you are the owner of the property, you can sell, mortgage, repair, and rent or lease option the property.

When you get the deed at a tax deed sale, you do not always get marketable title to the property immediately. In some cases, you still must perform a quiet title suit in which you must notify all the parties that have an interest in the property that the rights have been foreclosed out, and this can take up to six months to complete. Some other states require you to hold the title in escrow for six months to one year before recording to afford the owner the chance to redeem you out and get the property back. This is when the state has the sale of the tax deed with the right of redemption by the owner. In some other states, when the tax deed is issued, you now own the property outright and can do what you want with the property immediately, and the owner does *not* have any right of redemption.

CHAPTER 5

Strategy During Process

While you are waiting to get the title to the property in a tax lien foreclosure, you need to think about what your exit strategy will be. You also need to be aware that in some cases, the property tax lien will be redeemed by the property owner or subsequent tax lien holder before you get the ownership title to the property. If this happens, you end up with the return of your initial investment plus a preset interest rate as your profit. This interest rate can be as low as 8% per year to as high as 24% per year. You need to decide if you are looking for a fixed rate of return on your investment or you are looking to acquire property at a huge discount. The investment strategy used will be different based on what outcome you are looking for, and these strategies are as follows:

Interest Rate of Return

Let's say that you are looking for a fixed rate of return, so you need to pick the states that have the best interest rate for either tax liens or tax deeds with redemption. The only requirement to play in this arena is that you need to have the funds readily available because you need to pay in full the amount of your winning bid by the end of the day for the sale. That means if you bid $10,000 in tax liens, you need to have $10,000 in your account as you will be required to pay the tax collector by the end of the business day. So how can you be active in buying tax liens if you are like most beginning investors and lack sufficient cash to play in this arena? First, you need to step outside the box and think like a true investor-business person. If you know that you have the ability to purchase tax liens and consistently get 15% to 18% a year, could you not create an investment program where you promise to pay 10% to 13% per year to the investors who put up the capital? That would mean that you would get a 5% to 8% spread by using other people's money.

On May 31, 2006, I purchased a tax lien certificate numbered 06-017991 for $53.25 which was not a lot of money, but we need to consider the percent return. I won the bid with a certificate interest rate of 18%, and the owners have two years to pay. The tax lien certificate was redeemed (paid off) on July 26, 2006, and I received a check from the tax collector in the amount of $55.91. If you take the 55.91 (redemption amount) and divide by 53.25 (amount paid for the tax lien), you get a percent return on my investment of 5% (1.0499), but since it happened in two months, my actual annual return rate was 30%. Now, if you had invested, say, $10,000, and it redeems every two months, then in one year, that amount would have grown to roughly $13,400. If you were to use $100,000, then you would have earned over $34,000 that year which is a very good return.

LEE COUNTY TAX COLLECTOR

Check Write Date: 08/04/2006 August 4, 2006

Vendor: C0001933 145-54-5369 Thomas J Senatore

Certificate Number	Tax Year	Strap	Issue Date	Redeem Date	Interest Rate	Certificate Amount	Interest	Withheld	Total Due	Comment
06-017991	2005	27-46-27-00-00002.0010	05/31/2006	07/26/2006	18.00 %	$53.25	$2.66	$0.00	$55.91	Redemption
Certificate Total:						$53.25	$2.66	$0.00	$55.91	
Vendor Total:						$53.25	$2.66	$0.00	$55.91	

How does one start to create a private funding? One way would be to contact your accountant to see if they have any clients that have any low performing investments such as investments in the stock market. Why not educate your accountant so they can tell their clients how you can help them earn a better rate of return. As long as you can explain the tax lien process and how it works, you will not have much trouble getting others to invest with you.

Lee County Tax Collector
PO Box 850
Fort Myers, FL 33902
TELEPHONE (239) 533-6000
www.leetc.com

PAYABLE AT BANK OF AMERICA FT. MYERS, FL

CHECK NO. 202316

DATE August 4, 2006

AMOUNT *************55.91

PAY **** FIFTY FIVE AND 91/100

TO THE ORDER OF THOMAS J SENATORE
4916 SW 19TH PLACE
CAPE CORAL, FL 33914

Catherine M. Curtis
Authorized Signature

⑈202316⑈ ⑆063000047⑆ 00163950000 9⑈

This would be as long as they can see how they will get a better return on investment than they are getting now. Suppose you want to set up an investment pool of $500,000 which is a lot of money but possible to do. All you need to do is get ten people with $50,000 in an IRA account that is earning only 3% where you can promise them a 10% return. What do you think they would do?

Now you buy at a tax deed sale in Texas and earn 25% interest in six months if the owner redeems the tax deed, and your $500,000 investment is now worth $625.000. Now you invest the $625,000, and in six months, it is worth $781,250 one year after you started. Now it is time to pay the investors back the $500,000 plus the 10% interest of $50,000 which leaves $231,250 for you for putting the program together. This is based on the assumption that all of the tax deeds redeemed in the sixth month and you did not get any of the properties you purchased. If any of the tax deeds did not redeem, then the tax deed property could then be sold, and that would increase the amount of profit for a much higher rate of return.

Acquire and Hold Till Foreclosure Is Complete

Another way to profit is to purchase tax liens on less desirable properties such as board up buildings and vacant or abandoned properties that do not have the same demand that a nice home in a nice neighborhood would have. If we target properties that are not occupied, the chance that the owner will try to pay off (redeem) the tax lien is very slim. What I like to do is pick multiunit buildings in a low-income area that is starting to be revitalized and acquire these properties.

By getting these properties at a very low price, I will have the opportunity to make large profits. Now, we can either purchase the tax lien at the tax sale or we can buy existing tax liens from a third party, but either way, we end up with a tax lien that will eventually need to be foreclosed upon.

Now, we complete the foreclosure process and take title to the property which can take anywhere from six months to eighteen months.

Once we get the title to the property, there are a few things that you need to do immediately.

The first thing you need to do is to get insurance on your new investment to protect yourself in case someone gets injured on your property. The next thing to do is to physically inspect the property and make sure it is secure and determine which one of your several exit strategies you wish to pursue.

Your choice will be based on the neighborhood, the condition of the property, and your financial position at that time. You now have the opportunity to use one of the several basic investment strategies commonly used by investors, of which we have.

This property was purchased from the holder of the tax lien certificate and then was sold immediately after foreclosure was completed without doing any work to the property.

Sell "As Is" or Clean Up and Sell (Wholesale)

Now that you own the property, you can sell it in an "as is" condition, or you can sell it after you clean out the interior and clear up the yard.

The easiest thing to do is to create a prospectus on the property and hand it out at foreclosure sales, tax sales, and investor meetings. The easiest and quickest would be to sell the property as is, where is, and how is to an investor and not put any additional money into the property.

The only downside to this strategy is that you may be leaving some profit in the deal that you could get by putting a little time and effort into the property. Why not spend a little time and money to clean out the interior and the exterior of the property and get more money when you sell the property. The only problem if all you want to do is just sell the property fast is you may be losing $5,000 to $10,000 or more of potential profit.

I had one deal that I worked on that I got an addition $8,000 all because I cleaned out the junk from the interior of the property, cleaned up the front yard, and painted the exterior front of the house along the first floor to cover up the graffiti. Now that the property is cleared out, an investor can more easily visualize the finished project more so than if it were a mess. Now this may take some effort on your part and a few garbage containers.

All you have to do is hire a few laborers which should not cost you very much, and your rate of return will be much higher and will result with selling the property much faster.

How easy is it to find laborers you may ask? Most cities across the United States have day labor workers at inner city agencies. For those who are creative, you can always find individuals looking for a few hours of work outside of Home Depot or Lowes who work very for a fair wage.

The choice is always yours, and when in doubt, you can find contractors online who will clean out any type of property for you.

The tax lien foreclosure was completed on this property and then spent two days cleaning it up before it was sold.

Clean Up, Rehab, and Sell (Retail)

Now that you own the property, and it is all cleaned out, why not rehab the property and sell it for a much higher value? If you are qualified to do rehabs, you can do the work and get paid for your efforts.

Why not learn how to rehab properties and make this part of your overall business plan? Since you will not be spending all your time at the tax sales, you will need something to do with your spare time. I was fortunate in that I learned how to do home repairs and maintenance as a way to pay for my college education. Over the years, I learned how to do carpentry, masonry, electrics, roofing, spackling, painting, and plumbing work and eventually opened up my own construction company so I could pay myself to do some of the work.

But what if you are not handy at all like some of my friends are. what do you do? Then you need to have the funds to pay a contractor to do the work, or you may want to partner up with the contactor and split the profits with them when the property is sold.

If you can sell a property in an "as is" condition or in a remodeled condition, which one do you think you may have more buyers interested in buying the property? If you are dealing with single-family homes, you can sell the property to either an investor or homeowner.

Once you own the property, you also have the ability to sell the property on a lease option to a tenant buyer and help someone who typically could not qualify conventionally.

Clean Up, Rehab, and Keep as a Rental (Rentals)

Suppose you wish to be a landlord and are looking to acquire rental properties but lack the down payment or do not have the ability to get the mortgages needed. Why not buy a tax lien on a property where you only pay 1% to 3% of the value? You buy several tax liens and hope that one does not redeem and you get the title to the property. Now that you have the title to the property, you need to immediately start to remodel and get the unit(s) rented. If you do not have the funds to rehab, then you need to have other investors ready to loan you the rehab money, and when any of the tax liens redeem, you can use the money from that lien to cover the cost of the rehab loan. Once the building is in a livable condition, you now have the ability to refinance the property and pull more money out to buy additional tax liens. Now that you refinanced the property and have it rented out, you now have more residual income to buy more tax liens, and the process continues.

Acquire Right to Buy the Tax Lien and Assign Out for a Premium

An advanced strategy would be to look for tax liens on properties that are not in very good neighborhoods and see if the holder of the tax lien certificate would be willing to sell to you at a discount. In many instances, the holder of the certificate is looking for the redemption and not the property. When that is the case, you have the ability to ask for and get a discount from the certificate holder.

Now you need to find someone who may be in the market for a property in that condition and in that neighborhood.

How do you start to go about finding an investor to sell (or assign) your tax lien certificate to?

One easy way is to place an FSBO sign on the building and take down all the names and numbers of the investors and contractors who call you if you already have title to a property. Next, you place an online ad such as:

Motivated investor looking to sell a rehab property fast to a cash buyer. Please email me or call if interested. Have only a few properties left to sell.

Now that you have a list of investors and possibly contractors, you now can offer to sell the tax lien certificate to this new investor for a value slightly less than the face value which is going to be more than you have agreed to buy it for. The difference between your purchase price and the price paid by your new investor is your profit.

Let's say you find a property in the low-income section of town which is a boarded up three-family property with a tax lien at a total value of $35,439.21. You determine that the total lien is broken down to $17,500 in principle and $17,939.21 in interest.

Since the holder wants to get out and not take ownership of that property, you decide to offer $20,000 for the lien and close in thirty days or less. You now control a tax lien certificate with $15,439.21 in equity and decide to sell it to an investor/contractor for $32,000.00, leaving you with $12,000.00 in profit.

The investor/builder now has $3,439.21 in equity, and if it redeems before the tax lien is foreclosed, he will have made about 10% interest in less than twelve months (the time to complete the foreclosure).

The tax lien on this property was purchased and sold on the same day to another investor who was also a contractor for a profit of over $20,000 in a matter of hours, and we used the investor's money to do the entire deal so we had no money in the deal at all.

Acquire an Older Certificate and Wait to Be Redeemed Out

A favorite strategy of mine is to find properties with older tax lien certificates on it and buy those certificates. Be careful which states you do this because in some states, the tax lien certificate expires after a fixed amount of years, and you would be purchasing a worthless piece of paper. There are some states like Florida that when you request that the tax collector to start the foreclosure of your tax lien, you must pay off all existing tax liens. One thing to be careful is that the tax liens in Florida expire after seven years from the date they were issued. The advantage to this is that you may have obtained a tax lien with a low interest rate of say 6%, but your interest rate changes to 18% as soon as you request the foreclosure to be started. This could be a great strategy in Florida if you find a property that may be of interest and you buy the old certificate. Now you request the foreclosure to be started and then pay all the additional taxes liens, and you now get 18% on the entire amount, and the foreclosure process may take as long as twelve months.

For example, you find a tax certificate held by Lee County, Florida, and it is in the amount of $2,539.82 and was issued three years ago. You find out that there are three more tax liens which cover the subsequent years which total to $4,579.08. It will now cost you $7,118.90 of which you will be entitled to 1.5% per month till your lien is sold at a tax deed sale. You will, of course, have some processing fees to be paid of which you will earn interest on that money as well. In other tax lien states, the older tax lien holder has the right to redeem out (that means they have the right to pay off) the newer tax lien holder and add that amount to their tax lien. This will give you a better position and thus makes it more difficult for the owner to pay off the tax debt. The holder of the newer certificate has one of two choices, they can either allow you to redeem them out or they can pay you off. When you buy these tax lien certificates in some areas, these properties are desirable to investors and contractors, and they will try all ways to get these properties. What they do is find out what the total debt on the property is and determine if the maximum amount of debt on the property is within the range they need to be a good deal.

An example of this may be a duplex in a low-income/moderate-income area that is in need of rehab. The total amount of tax liens equal $18,500, and the repairs are estimated at $65,000, for a total investment of $83,500. If the property in the area that is comparable sells for $80,000 to $85,000 and rent for only $400 per month (each unit), you may not want to get this property unless the appreciation or growth is on the upswing. Now, if the price range is $90,000 to $120,000 and the rents are greater than $500 per month, then run, don't walk, as this is a good deal.

How to Purchase

Another strategy which I used most often when I first started out was to get lists from the big companies of the tax liens they were looking to unload. I would look for those tax liens that were more than two years old and were ready to start the foreclosure process or the ones that were already in the foreclosure process. The reason being was that I did not have a lot of cash to buy these, so I had to get partners and share in the profits. My partners did not want to wait two to three years for us to buy a tax lien and wait two years to do our own foreclosure, so I had to pick and choose the ones I thought would move quickly through the legal court system. I spent some time looking for potential deals and found several properties in the low-income neighborhoods of Jersey City, New Jersey, that were owned by Transamerica Business Credit Corp that they would sell for a discount. I then discovered that this company had several properties that they had started the tax line foreclosure process on and were close to completing the foreclosure process but did not want to take title because of the condition of the neighborhood. Since I was able to get several properties at a discount, I found my niche in the system where I could buy these at a discount and then assign the tax sale certificate I purchased from them to another investor. I would sell the same tax sale certificate to these investors for a value more than I agreed to pay and was slightly lower than the actual value and make my profit on the spread. The investors I did the deals with would make their profit if the tax sale certificate were to be redeemed by the owner or another lien holder or they got the property and sold it for an even larger profit. As the desire for property in this area grew and more investors were attracted to this city, I had to change my strategy and adjust with the demand. I found that I had to buy all the older tax sale certificates because other investors had found out about the demand and growth that had taken over the city and were trying to get any properties they could. As the demand increased, I had to again change my strategy as evident by the following. In 2002–2003, I purchased a three-family home that was listed in the newspaper just a few blocks from a property I got from a tax lien two years earlier. I paid $150,000 for this property which had tax liens and was in foreclosure. I had to put some money into this property during the time it was rented out and sold it three years later for over $ 300,000.

OCT 10 2000 14:06 FR TMF 5618422946 TO 12013421618 P.04/24

Schedule "A"

Assignment Quote for TAD, Inc.

Owner: Av Monticello
Owner Address: 581 Jersey Ave
Jersey City, NJ 07302-242

Certificate Number: 205350
Parcel ID: 1920-18.A
Block/Lot: 1920/18.A
Property Address: 191-191A Monticello Ave.
Jersey City, NJ 07304-2534

A0108000229
A0166000419

	AccrualDate:	LienAmount:	Interest Rate:	Accrued Interest:
Lien Detail:	02/26/1997	$3,286.20	18.00%	$2,242.18
Subsequents:	02/26/1997	$20,122.19	18.00%	$13,326.95
	05/16/1997	$681.41	18.00%	$424.75
	12/18/1998	$1,497.03	18.00%	$504.23
Cert. #252111	06/11/1998	$2,990.24	18.00%	$1,347.16
	03/31/1999	$727.02	18.00%	$207.95
	Total:	$29,304.09		$18,053.22

	Fee Date:	Fee Type:	Fee Amount:	Fee Interest:
FeeDetail:	02/26/1997	Recording Fee	$3.19	$0.00
	07/14/1999	Legal Fee	$222.50	$0.00
	09/03/1999	Recording Fee	$10.50	$0.00
	12/10/1999	Title Search Fee	$250.00	$0.00
		Total:	$486.19	$0.00

Payoff Valid Through:	10/31/2000
Total Lien Amount:	$29,304.09
Total Interest:	$18,053.22
Total Fees:	$486.19
Subtotal:	$47,843.50
Total Payments:	$0.00
Total Due:	$25,000.00

Payment Instructions: *Please Make Check Payable To:* *Transamerica Business Credit Corp*
Remit To: *630 U.S. Highway # 1, Suite 300*
North Palm Beach, FL 33408
Attention: Neil J. Harreveld

10/10/00

Sample tax lien property:

The picture on the preceding page is an example of a property that I acquired by way of a *tax lien*. The tax lien on this property was held by a company who was known as Transamerica Business Credit Corp (Transamerica) located in West Palm Beach, Florida. They would go out and buy tax liens in bulk volume and acquired several thousand tax liens over the years. What I did on this deal was to purchase a tax lien from a third party on a property that they have already started the foreclosure process on and were close to completion of that foreclosure.

I received a list from Transamerica which detailed the address and the amount of the tax lien. I went out to the neighborhood where this property was located only to find out it was located in a rough low-income neighborhood. The brick building looked solid from the exterior and, based on the location and the view from the road, probably needed a lot of work on the interior. The full amount of the tax lien including the tax, interest, legal fees, and processing fees came out to be $47,843.50. Based on my research and knowledge of the neighborhood, I felt that the property had a value in its current condition of $90,000. The property was estimated to need close to $100,000 in repairs and believed I could renovate the property in seven to nine months.

Now comes the interesting part of making offers on a property, the *negotiations*. I decided to start my offer at $20,000 in order to get a reaction from the seller. Just as I expected, my offer was declined, but what I did not expect was that they agreed to sell the tax lien to me at a purchase price of $25,000. When I got the breakdown from Transamerica, I discovered that they had $29,304.09 in actual money spent and $18,053.24 in interest which gave the tax lien certificate a face value of $47,843.50. This made the deal even better because if the property owner decided to redeem the tax lien certificate before I got the foreclosure completed, I would have made $22,843.50 in profit. The foreclosure process was only thirty days from completion, and if the property owner redeemed the tax lien certificate within that time, I would have had a profit rate of 91% ROI. (Return on investment is derived by taking the amount of profit divided by the amount of the purchase.) This would be the (profit) 22,843.50 divided by (cost) 25,000 which is as follows: 22,843.50/25,000 = 91%. Now, this ROI is derived based on the tax lien certificate being redeemed in the firs thirty days which means the annual ROI would have been 1092%.

Now that I got you interested, I need to tell you what happened. I had my attorney, Michael Pellegrino, who was working on the tax lien foreclosure for Transamerica to now complete it for me. He got the foreclosure completed and sent me a copy of the signed final judgment which was my deed to the property in late December. I now had to check inspect my property and found that there were four apartments and two storefronts. The entire building needed to be remodeled starting with the large hole in the roof. Being it was winter, I had to first patch the roof and then get heat to the building.

The repairs included electrical, plumbing, kitchens, and bathrooms for starters and nine months, and +/– $80,000 later, my building was 100% remodeled and was rented with a cash flow of $4,500/month. I now had $105,000 invested and in one year refinanced the property and got back $100,000 which was now tax-free since it was a mortgage. Five years after I obtained the building, it was sold for $540,000 with a total profit including rents of almost one million dollars.

Locating Money Sources

Private Money

There are several ways to gather money for the purchase of tax liens and tax deeds. The most basic and easiest way is to use private money. Private money is the funding by an individual who would like to get a better return on their money than they are getting right now. The average person is typically earning 3%–5% on their investments because they are using the traditional vehicles such as the stock market. The interest rate you will pay these private lenders vary and could be as low as 8% and as high as 12%, but this is much better then hard money lenders. The other advantage is that the private money lender may lend up to 100% of the entire deal and not have many extra fees.

You may ask, how can I get "private money" if I am just starting out buying tax liens? Well, the first thing I need to do is to get into the right frame of mind. Remember that attitude is a major factor and the second would be knowledge, and only then would experience follow. If you go up to someone and you present yourself as a knowledgeable investor, they will feel comfortable with you. Then, if you are able to explain how the system of tax liens and tax deeds work, you will have an even greater chance they will invest with you. What you are doing is to appeal to their desire for unlimited amounts or wealth.

What I like to do is meet with a person several times before we even discuss money because I want them to feel comfortable with me.

When you sit down with the investor, do not try to be cautious with telling them about how this works because you need to build trust. What I have done is I worked with a few people over the years to help fund my purchases, and I agreed to split the profits evenly. One such investor that funded my deals is Dallas and now is one of my closest friends. We started out with small deals, and over the years, as our comfort level increased, so did the amount he would entrust to me for investing. Remember that trust in this business and reputation and honor are the most important factors when dealing with people.

Now the most important question you may ask is not what private money is, not how it works, but rather how do I find someone to give me the money to do the deals. First of all, everyone has an accountant or knows an accountant. What if you educate that person as to what you do or what you want to do? They could then refer some of clients of theirs that may have some money earning low interest over to you to invest and make them much higher interest rates. I have used my accountant for several leads as well as many others that I found through my daily activities every day. You will be surprised how many potential private money lenders come across every day that you pass up. You know what they say, you will make it in this business by the people you meet and the hands you shake. When you're out each and every day, you need to talk to people and let them know what you do because that is the best way to find people to fund your deals. One such person is Dr. Mazejy, a dentist who was referred to me by a close friend. We went in on a deal in Fair Lawn, New Jersey, on two four-unit buildings we decided to buy for $500,000, all cash, and we used his cash as well as another partner we brought into the deal. After a few months, we decided that the two should buy me out, and I was paid to leave the partnership that all I had into it was my time and knowledge.

It is always nice to have money, but it is more important to have the knowledge and the ability to use that knowledge because more doors will open up for you when there were only obstacles. Another way was on an airplane sitting next to someone. I introduced myself and just started talking to them about what I do and that I am always looking to help others, and now they are in my database. What you need to do is be able to write down on paper what returns someone can expect if they are going to invest with you. You need to be able to show what and how the profits will be obtained and be able to explain that to another individual. What most people look for in ROI (return on investment) and when can they expect to be paid.

Hard Money

This is very much similar to private money with the following differences. The way this works is that once you have a deal pending, you contact the hard money lender and show them the deal. They will look over the numbers, the area where the property is located, and then they will want to look over your financials. If they are still interested in lending you the money, they will lend you only 65% to 75% with an interest rate of 12% to 16%, and they may charge you one to four points (one point equals 1% of the loan amount). With the evolution of investing, the way hard money lenders work has changed as well. It used to be where they would only look at the deal and then lend you the money, but now, they look at you the person to be sure you are not financially strapped. There are several ways to find these lenders, and the simplest way would be to use the Internet. You could search by using the keyword "hard money lending" and will be given an extensive list of lenders.

Another way would be to see a mortgage broker as they often have a list of these lenders. You can also go to an investor club meeting and see if anyone there is a hard money lender. There are usually several members that have been very successful as a real estate investor and now just lend their money out at the high interest rates. Today's hard money lenders were yesterday's real estate investors.

Negotiating with Any Prior Lien Holder for Their Lien

One of the advanced buying strategies would be to find older lien holders on a property that you may be interested in obtaining.

Let's say you find a property that you may be interested in, and then you find out that there is a tax lien on the property. What you need to do is find out who the tax lien holder is and try to buy their tax lien certificate. To find out who the holder of the tax lien certificate is, you can start by asking the tax collector. Now that you know who this person is, you need to contact them to see if they are willing to sell their certificate to you. What may be their reason for selling their certificate to you? In many instances, the small investor will buy a lot more tax lien certificates than they can handle or afford to maintain when they have to pay the subsequent taxes (these are the taxes that become due after you purchased the tax lien certificate).

What you need to do is evaluate the deal to see the total amount of the subsequent taxes on that property. In most cases, the total amount due for all of the taxes is still less than 20% of the total value of the property. Once you acquire an older tax lien certificate, you need to pay off all of the subsequent tax liens, and that amount will now merge into your tax lien value which you now can start the foreclosure on with the higher dollar value. I also found out that many of the larger companies that purchase the tax liens in the billions of dollars often need to liquidate some of their portfolio in order to buy more tax liens. I have done several deals with large players in this business by purchasing their tax liens at a discount and then sell the tax liens to another investor. Why not use the wholesaling techniques you have and then use them in the area of tax liens?

Work on "How to Complete the Paperwork"

There are going to be times when the paperwork needs to be completed in a timely fashion that we covered in chapter 2. With that being said, I will let you know that it is probably in your best interest that you use an attorney to process your tax lien foreclosure instead of you. They know the law much better than you and understand how the process works. The best part is if they make a mistake or miss a time deadline that they know how to correct their mistake, and it will not cost you any additional funds. If you do it on your own, then you are solely responsible for your errors. When you go to a tax sale, the tax collector will have the paperwork that needs to be completed before the sale starts. After the sale, there are also things that need to be completed that are just as important. The first thing is the tax lien certificate needs to be recorded with the county clerk as a lien on the property.

The reason we do this is to protect your claim against the property should the owner sell the property to a third party. Because this tax lien is recorded with the county clerk, register of deeds, or the "prothonotary" office as they call it in Pennsylvania, in any case, it will be found when the title company does the title search and prepares a title insurance policy. The lien will be listed in the title insurance exceptions and will be the responsibility of the new owner to ensure that the lien is paid off. My background as a paralegal was extensive in tax liens, and I know how to process the tax lien foreclosure, but I still use attorneys to do the foreclosure for me. First of all, my time is better utilized not doing the paperwork but rather finding the deals. Second is that the attorney is insured and is responsible to get the foreclosure done in a timely manner.

"Lease Option" Deals

What is "lease option," and what does it have to do with tax liens and tax deeds? Well the answer is simple: having a tax lien on your property is a circumstance. As a matter of fact, it is a huge circumstance, and you can use it to get into a deal. If a person has a tax lien on their property, they are probably in debt and have financial difficulties. What we can do is offer to take over their property and have them sell us the property on a long-term lease at an agreed upon price today and close in the near future. What we are doing is helping the homeowner get out from under that huge financial burden and give them the immediate relief they are looking for. We now control the property and get into the deal by paying off the tax lien which becomes our deposit money to the owner. Now that we control the property and have removed it from the tax sale, we can now fix up the property enough to get it rented to a new tenant buyer, or we can just sell it outright to a potential homeowner. At this point, we would have the ability to almost anything with the property, and we did not have to qualify for a mortgage or come out of pocket for any substantial down payment.

One thing you may want to do with the seller is to have a power of attorney as to the deed, or we have the seller put the deed into escrow with their attorney or my attorney. This way, when the time comes to close, we do not have any problems with the transfer of title. In most cases, it will be advantageous to have the owner get some money at closing to ensure that they show up. What we do here is set up this transaction where all involved feel like they won, and now the deal was set up for success.

Paperwork for "Lease Option"

There are going to be several documents needed for you to do the lease option with the property owner. As with any legal documents, I always recommend that you have your local attorney review them before they are used as you want to make sure they comply with all your state rules and regulations. The first of many things we need is to get an "authorization to release information" so that we can contact the mortgage company that the owner has their mortgage with to see what the balance is. The next thing we need is a single contract for the "lease agreement with a purchase option." This is basically a residential lease agreement that details the terms of the rental, but it also has a section where it stipulates that you have the ability or option to purchase the property at a fixed price and before a fixed date. You will also need to have them sign a disclaimer and disclosure which explains to all parties as to what and how we are doing this lease option deal. These are legal documents that if you are not sure of what you are doing, you use an attorney to process the paperwork for you. There are several books on how to do lease options as well as there are several companies out there that teach the process, and most all tell you that you should use an attorney to do all the contacts. One of the real estate education companies that teach lease options very well is the "Wealth Intelligence Academy" located in Cape Coral, Florida, and teaches three-day seminars on this subject and others all around the country and abroad.

What to Do with the Money

Now that your tax lien or tax deed deal is completed and you got paid, what should we do with the money? The first thing to do is to reinvest the money quickly to have it work for you. One thing you need to remember is that if you keep turning over your money, you will build up your wealth much faster than if you spent the profits on doodads. If you're using another investor's money, then you really need to have another deal for them to reinvest because if you don't, they may take their money elsewhere. I like to keep investing the profits and not spend it now but later. If I am getting 18% to 25% return, and I am splitting that with my investor, and then I will have to do many deals before I have enough money to invest on my own. I believe that if I work hard now, I can enjoy it all later. The first thing you need to do is write down your plan and then make it happen.

CHAPTER 6

The Profit Process

How to Resell Your Property in Less than Thirty Days

Step 1: The Tax Sale Auction

Before we can get to the profit, we need to first get to the deal. We will look over the list of tax sales for the month and find a tax sale we would like to attend. Below is a copy of the list that can be found on our website in the member's only section.

This is the list for July 28 that I attended online.

State	Jurisdiction	Type	Date	Time
07/28/09				
AR	Crittenden County	DEED	07/28/09	
FL	Bay County	DEED	07/28/09	
FL	Broward County	DEED	07/28/09	
FL	Charlotte County	DEED	07/28/09	
FL	Jackson County	DEED	07/28/09	
FL	Lake County	DEED	07/28/09	
FL	Nassau County	DEED	07/28/09	
FL	Osceola County	DEED	07/28/09	
FL	Washington County	DEED	07/28/09	
IA	Linn County	SHERIFF	07/28/09	
IA	Woodbury County	SHERIFF	07/28/09	
IN	Kosciusko County	SHERIFF	07/28/09	
IN	Marshall County	SHERIFF	07/28/09	
ME	Town of Sumner	DEED	07/28/09	
MI	Lenawee County	DEED	07/28/09	
MI	Macomb County	DEED	07/28/09	
NM	Taos County	DEED	07/28/09	
NV	City of Las Vegas	LIEN	07/28/09	
NV	City of North Las Vegas	LIEN	07/28/09	
NY	Village of Bayville	DEED	07/28/09	

As I look over the list, I see a category for *type* which will indicate whether the sale is a tax lien sale, tax deed sale, or a sheriff sale. I am looking for the tax deed sales and see that Florida has several on the same day. I do some research and find that Charlotte County has good property values and many parcels on the list.

I now need to do additional research to see what if any I want to possibly purchase. There are two different sites I can go to.

The first is the tax lien website shown below:

The second is the tax deed website shown below:

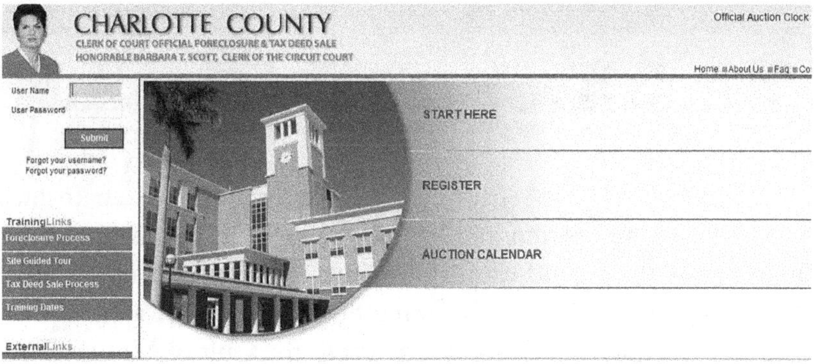

Both are for the county but have different sales. I will log into the tax deed site and see what properties they have available. When I am registered and have made my deposit by ACH, I am now ready to begin the bidding. Just a quick note, in Charlotte County, you have to have the entire amount of the winning bid paid in full by 9:00 a.m. the next day. If you do not pay the funds on time, you then risk the chance of being eliminated from future sales. I can, however, place enough money in the ACH to cover the entire purchase amount and designate the payment by way of the ACH deposit made in advance.

Let's take a look at the bid page:

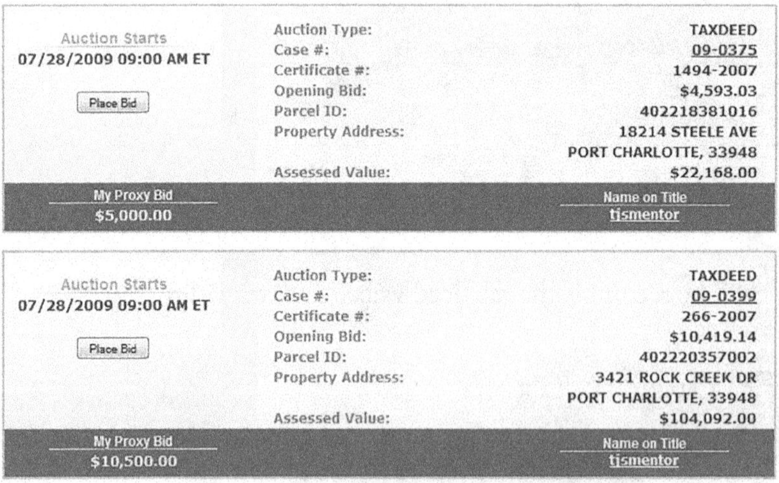
Auction Starts
07/28/2009 09:00 AM ET
Place Bid

Auction Type:	TAXDEED
Case #:	09-0375
Certificate #:	1494-2007
Opening Bid:	$4,593.03
Parcel ID:	402218381016
Property Address:	18214 STEELE AVE PORT CHARLOTTE, 33948
Assessed Value:	$22,168.00

My Proxy Bid $5,000.00
Name on Title tjsmentor

Auction Starts
07/28/2009 09:00 AM ET
Place Bid

Auction Type:	TAXDEED
Case #:	09-0399
Certificate #:	266-2007
Opening Bid:	$10,419.14
Parcel ID:	402220357002
Property Address:	3421 ROCK CREEK DR PORT CHARLOTTE, 33948
Assessed Value:	$104,092.00

My Proxy Bid $10,500.00
Name on Title tjsmentor

Here are two properties I found that were of interest to me, and I have set an opening bid for each parcel. The first is of limited interest, but the second was of high interest. The property at 3421 Rock Creek Drive is a single-family house located on a canal that goes into Charlotte Harbor and then into the Gulf of Mexico. This is a desirable property.

When you start to bid, you will be asked to confirm the next four screens which will give the county a release of any liability.

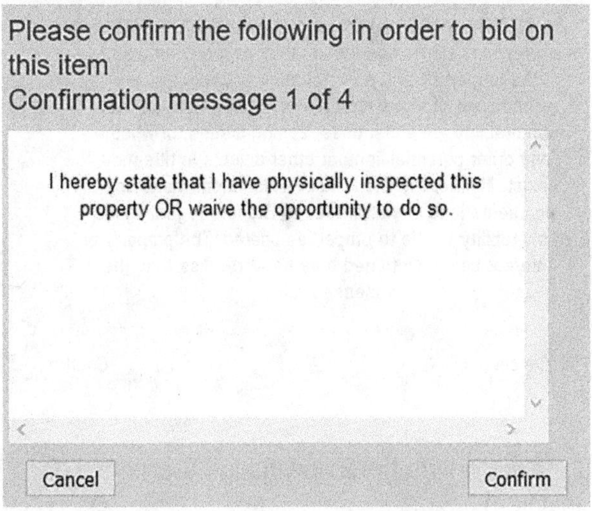
Please confirm the following in order to bid on this item
Confirmation message 1 of 4
I hereby state that I have physically inspected this property OR waive the opportunity to do so.
Cancel
Confirm

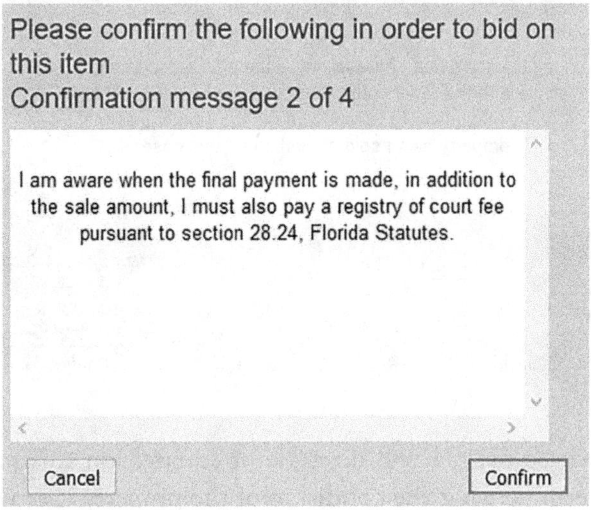
Please confirm the following in order to bid on this item
Confirmation message 2 of 4
I am aware when the final payment is made, in addition to the sale amount, I must also pay a registry of court fee pursuant to section 28.24, Florida Statutes.
Cancel
Confirm

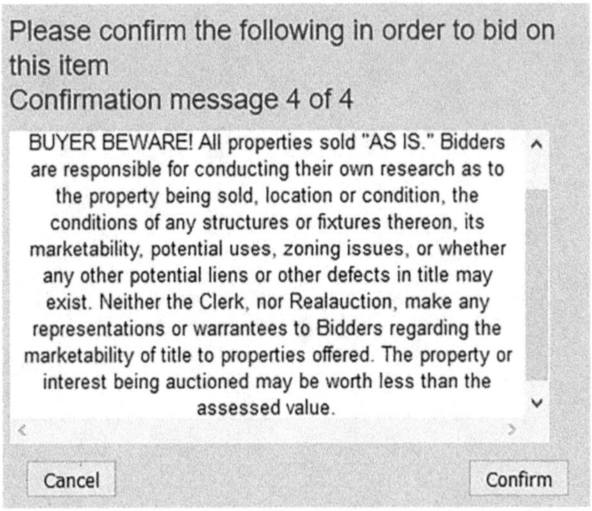

Please confirm the following in order to bid on this item
Confirmation message 4 of 4

BUYER BEWARE! All properties sold "AS IS." Bidders are responsible for conducting their own research as to the property being sold, location or condition, the conditions of any structures or fixtures thereon, its marketability, potential uses, zoning issues, or whether any other potential liens or other defects in title may exist. Neither the Clerk, nor Realauction, make any representations or warrantees to Bidders regarding the marketability of title to properties offered. The property or interest being auctioned may be worth less than the assessed value.

Cancel Confirm

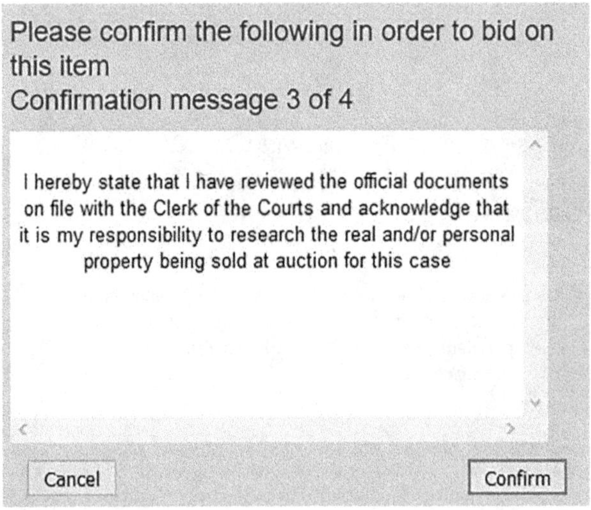

Please confirm the following in order to bid on this item
Confirmation message 3 of 4

I hereby state that I have reviewed the official documents on file with the Clerk of the Courts and acknowledge that it is my responsibility to research the real and/or personal property being sold at auction for this case

Cancel Confirm

So what's next? I will do a bit of research on this parcel and try to determine what the condition of the property is as well as the neighborhood. I go to the Internet to find out the property location and pull the house up on Google. I then will check out the home values on Trulia and Zillow. I will then try to see what advantages the property has to offer and what demand *if any* there might be.

An aerial view of the property location:

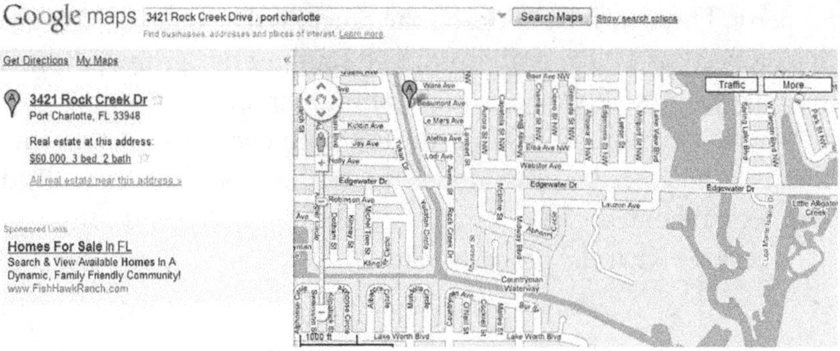

From this photo, I see that the property is on a main canal that leads into the bay and then off to the river and gulf. This can be listed as a gulf access property which will provide the additional means to resell quickly.

I also notice that there are two bridges to pass under which will eliminate sailboat access to the property.

Although this is a negative, the positive is that a boat up to thirty feet could possibly pass under the bridge which is great.

Let's see what a close up of the home reveals:

As we see from this photo of this house and property, the home is surrounded by larger homes which will increase the value of this property. There are boat docks on the canal for the homes adjacent to this property as well as both north and south of this property which indicate the uses of boats are quite common in this area.

The waterway (canal) is wide and deep enough to handle any boat that may need to pass under the bridge, and the area is filled with several homes.

Let's see what the property values are.

3421 Rock Creek Dr Port Charlotte FL 33948
-- beds, 2.0 baths, 903 sq ft

Zestimate®: $102,500 ?

My Estimate: CREATE

Monthly Payment: $ 449 EDIT **Current Rates**

Need to refi? Don't lock in without checking Zillow first.

Bird's Eye View ADD | EDIT PHOTOS

▸ See a Street View or larger Bird's Eye View for 3421 Rock Creek Dr

Based on Zillow, the property has a value of $102,500 and is truly one of the smaller homes, while the other homes in the area are selling for much more money, so this is a great deal if the price is right. With all the information I have viewed, the next step is to see the front of the property, and that can be obtained from the Internet as well.

Here is a front view of the property.

This property has much going for it, and from all the data so far, I am interested in bidding on this property. I need to rely on much of the information I can obtain online if I am looking to invest long distance. Many investors would not even attempt to bid on this property if they did not live in Charlotte County, Florida.

My hope is that when you have completed this book and understood what I have done, your fears will be gone forever. I have not physically seen this property nor have I been in that neighborhood. So my entire deal was done as a distant investor. I could have been in Los Angeles, Australia, or London, it does not matter. The entire process was done from my laptop.

So let's see what the next step will bring.

Step 2: What Are My Exit Strategies?

Here is what I have to work with.

The home has a western exposure, so the sun will be in the front in the afternoons and in the rear in the mornings. That would mean the sunrise and water are on the same side, good marketing value.

I guess I would have to look over the options and see which of the exit strategies would work the best to fit my needs. If I were a beginning investor, I would probably base my strategy of the quickest return.

1. Quick Turn Strategy: When I get the home and want to resell it quickly, what purchase price would I need to be at for a basis? What are the surrounding home sale values, and can I be well below that price? When I win the bid, can I sell it at a value of 50% below current market value? As an investor, this one would most likely be my first choice. So I run the numbers to see:
   a. Current market value: $109,000, CMV
   b. After repair value: $149,000, ARV
   c. Repair costs: $ 20,000
   d. Repair timetable: sixty days
   e. Market rents: $900 per month

   If I were to work all the numbers, I would end up with a purchase price in the range of $60,000 to $80,000 for this property. I know that as an investor, these are the numbers I would pay for a property like this in a neighborhood similar to the one here.
2. Retail Strategy: When I get the property, what will be the cost to remodel the home to sell for top dollar? Will the home require major or minor work? Do I have to do the work myself, or can I afford to hire someone? How long will all the work take?
   a. Again, we look at the same numbers.
   b. Cost to advertise would be 1% to 6% of the sale price.
   c. Buy for $60,000, add $20,000, and the basis would be $80,000.

   d. Can sell below ARV, say at $120,000.
   e. Should take thirty to ninety days.
   f. That would be a return of 40%.
3. Rental Strategy: When I get the property, what will be the best rents I can get for a home like this? What will be the cost to remodel the home? Will the home require major or minor work? Do I have to do the work myself, or can I afford to hire someone? How long will all the work take?
   a. Again, we look at the same numbers.
   b. Cost to advertise would be one month's rent.
   c. Buy for $60,000, add $20,000, and the basis would be $80,000.
   d. Current possible rent of $900 per month; that is $10,800 annually.
   e. That would be a return of 13.5%.
4. Lease Option/Vendor Finance Strategy: When I get the property, what will be the best rents I can get for a home like this? How long do I want to rent it out for? What would be the sale price based on this strategy? What will be the cost to remodel the home? Will the home require major or minor work? Do I have to do the work myself, or can I afford to hire someone? How long will all the work take?
   a. Again, we look at the same numbers.
   b. Cost to advertise would be one month's rent.
   c. Buy for $60,000, add $20,000, and the basis would be $80,000.
   d. Current possible rent of $900 per month; that is $10,800 annually.
   e. Least option price would be at $160,000 in three years.
   f. Total profit would be $112,400.
   g. That would be a return of 181%.

Just to recap my exit options at a glance:

Strategy	Profit
Flip the property quickly in thirty days or less:	$10,000.00
Sell to homeowner after remodel completed:	$40,000.00
Should take ninety days or less	
Remodel and hold as a rental:	$600/month
Lease option/vendor finance:	$600/month
Net profit when closed in three years	$112,000.00

Step 3: What Is the Bid Process?

Now, when we have decided that this has potential, we need to take the next step and bid on the property. We go to the bid page, and we see that the auction details are listed on the bid page shown below.

I can go to the "Place Bid" box, click on it, and place my bid. I placed my bid of $10,500 as the opening bid was $10,419.14. If no other bidders came forward, the property would be mine for the opening bid amount. The auction started at 9:00 a.m. EST as indicated on the bid box. On the twenty-eighth, at 8:50 a.m., I logged into the site to see the auction take place in live time. The way this auction works is that upon the opening of the auction, it will show the bottom bar of that listed property with either, "You have the highest bid" or "you have been outbid"; in either case, the auction clock is shown, and as long as you're the highest bidder and not outbid, the clock runs down. If you are outbid, then the clock will reset with sixty to ninety seconds more. At the conclusion of the auction, you will be notified of the results and be given instructions as the successful bidder.

You also receive a follow-up phone call to congratulate you on being the successful bidder.

Below are the results from the sale:

Sale Date	Case ID	Bidder	Winning Bid	Deposit	Auction Balance	Clerk Fees	Rec Fees	EA Fee	Doc ** Stamps	Total Due
07/28/2009	09-0496	6258	$2,000.00	$200.00	$1,800.00	$0.00	$35.50	$0.00	$14.00	**$1,849.50**
07/28/2009	09-0485	6153	$2,200.00	$200.00	$2,000.00	$0.00	$35.50	$0.00	$15.40	**$2,050.90**
07/28/2009	09-0484	5071	$2,300.00	$200.00	$2,100.00	$0.00	$35.50	$0.00	$16.10	**$2,151.60**
07/28/2009	09-0478	6309	$5,300.00	$200.00	$5,100.00	$0.00	$35.50	$0.00	$37.10	**$5,172.60**
07/28/2009	09-0470	n/a	$1,898.36	$0.00	$0.00	$0.00	$0.00	$0.00	$0.00	**$0.00**
07/28/2009	09-0469	n/a	$1,930.84	$0.00	$0.00	$0.00	$0.00	$0.00	$0.00	**$0.00**
07/28/2009	09-0468	n/a	$3,547.15	$0.00	$0.00	$0.00	$0.00	$0.00	$0.00	**$0.00**
07/28/2009	09-0467	5229	$3,700.00	$200.00	$3,500.00	$0.00	$35.50	$0.00	$25.90	**$3,561.40**
07/28/2009	09-0466	5229	$1,900.00	$200.00	$1,700.00	$0.00	$35.50	$0.00	$13.30	**$1,748.80**
07/28/2009	09-0441	5506	$3,200.00	$200.00	$3,000.00	$0.00	$35.50	$0.00	$22.40	**$3,057.90**
07/28/2009	09-0433	6162	$20,500.00	$200.00	$20,300.00	$0.00	$35.50	$0.00	$143.50	**$20,479.00**
07/28/2009	09-0416	5574	$2,100.00	$200.00	$1,900.00	$0.00	$35.50	$0.00	$14.70	**$1,950.20**
07/28/2009	09-0413	6251	$6,100.00	$200.00	$5,900.00	$0.00	$35.50	$0.00	$42.70	**$5,978.20**
07/28/2009	09-0403	5218	$2,700.00	$200.00	$2,500.00	$0.00	$35.50	$0.00	$18.90	**$2,554.40**
07/28/2009	09-0402	5506	$3,400.00	$200.00	$3,200.00	$0.00	$35.50	$0.00	$23.80	**$3,259.30**
07/28/2009	09-0399	6049	$42,600.00	$200.00	$42,400.00	$0.00	$35.50	$0.00	$298.20	**$42,733.70**
07/28/2009	09-0398	5506	$2,500.00	$200.00	$2,300.00	$0.00	$35.50	$0.00	$17.50	**$2,353.00**
07/28/2009	09-0390	5071	$2,300.00	$200.00	$2,100.00	$0.00	$35.50	$0.00	$16.10	**$2,151.60**
07/28/2009	09-0366	5116	$2,300.00	$200.00	$2,100.00	$0.00	$35.50	$0.00	$16.10	**$2,151.60**
07/28/2009	09-0360	6251	$2,500.00	$200.00	$2,300.00	$0.00	$35.50	$0.00	$17.50	**$2,353.00**
07/28/2009	09-0303	6049	$3,200.00	$200.00	$3,000.00	$0.00	$35.50	$0.00	$22.40	**$3,057.90**
07/28/2009	09-0302	6049	$3,100.00	$200.00	$2,900.00	$0.00	$35.50	$0.00	$21.70	**$2,957.20**

As you can clearly see, there were twenty-two properties sold that day, and when you look over the list, you will see all the bidders who won properties that day. When you find bidder number 6049, you will find the three properties I purchased.

Below is the screen at the conclusion of that parcel sale:

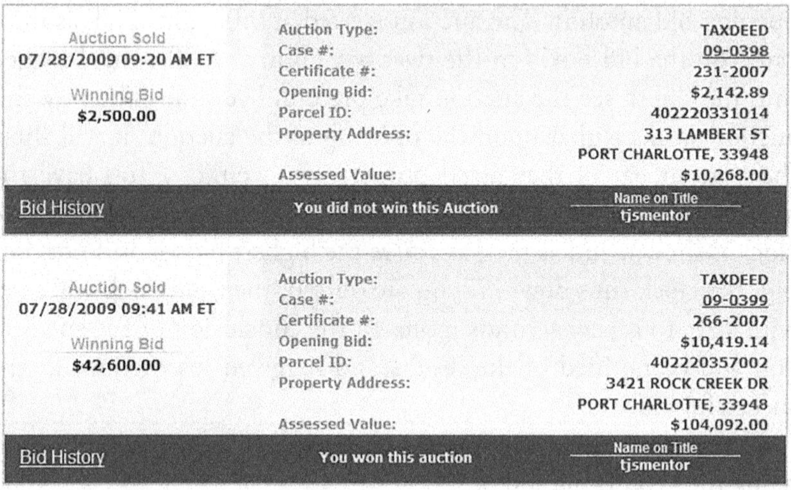

Auction Sold	Auction Type:	TAXDEED
07/28/2009 09:20 AM ET	Case #:	09-0398
	Certificate #:	231-2007
Winning Bid	Opening Bid:	$2,142.89
$2,500.00	Parcel ID:	402220331014
	Property Address:	313 LAMBERT ST
		PORT CHARLOTTE, 33948
	Assessed Value:	$10,268.00
Bid History	You did not win this Auction	Name on Title tjsmentor

Auction Sold	Auction Type:	TAXDEED
07/28/2009 09:41 AM ET	Case #:	09-0399
	Certificate #:	266-2007
Winning Bid	Opening Bid:	$10,419.14
$42,600.00	Parcel ID:	402220357002
	Property Address:	3421 ROCK CREEK DR
		PORT CHARLOTTE, 33948
	Assessed Value:	$104,092.00
Bid History	You won this auction	Name on Title tjsmentor

As you can see from the previous page, I purchased the parcel for $42,600. My limit was to go as high as $60,000, so I actually saved money that day. Since I purchased the property for far below the price I was estimating, the exit strategy possibilities just got larger. My goal will be to reclaim the money I paid in the shortest amount of time.

But I left one thing out. Now that I won the bid, I need to pay for it. In Charlotte County, they have three ways in which you can pay. I could either use the money I have on account, complete a bank wire transfer, or bring the money into the tax collector's office. I did not have that much on account, so I had to get the money into the office. As a Florida resident, I am permitted to use a local bank drawn check, so I had the check dropped off first thing Wednesday morning.

I now had to wait only three days before I got the deed from the county.

TAX DEED

State of Florida
County Of Charlotte

The following Tax Sale Certificate Numbered 266-2007 issued on 31st day of May, 2007 was filed in the office of the Tax Collector of this County and application made for the issuance of a tax deed, the applicant having paid or redeemed all other taxes or tax sale certificates on the land described as required by law to be paid or redeemed, and the costs and expenses of this sale, and due notice of sale having been published as required by law, and no person entitled to do so having appeared to redeem said land; such land was sold on the 28th day of July, 2009, offered for sale as required by law for cash to the highest bidder and was sold to:
Thomas J Senatore

ADDRESS:

being the highest bidder and having paid the sum of his bid as required by the Laws of Florida.

NOW, on 28th day of July, 2009, in the County of Charlotte, State of Florida, in consideration of the sum of 42,600.00 Forty-two thousand six hundred dollars only being the amount paid pursuant to the Laws of Florida does hereby sell the following lands, including any hereditaments, buildings, fixtures and improvements of any kind and description, situated in the County and State aforesaid and described as follows:
PCH 008 0216 0053 PORT CHARLOTTE
SEC 8 BLK 216 LT 53
Original Owners of Record:
GALUSKA, JOHN J.
GALUSKA, HELEN S.

Barbara T. Scott
Clerk of the Circuit Court or County Comptroller

Witness:
CAROLINE HUMPHRIES
NANCY E. LANE

By: DEBORAH F. BACHANT, Deputy Clerk

State of Florida

Step 4: First Thing to Do After Winning the Bid

The first thing you do is tell yourself, *Good job!*

Now you are ready to get this property insured. Contact your insurance agent and advise them you just purchased a home and you would like to get it insured. You typically would get a liability insurance policy and a structure policy.

The limits for liability are up to you, but the structure will usually be at replacement cost, and that runs around $1,000 for the year. Since I am looking to resell fast, the insurance will be only limited to a few days to a few weeks.

Check with your insurance agent. You may be covered when you buy property in your residence state. I like to buy the property and then contact my agent to get a policy over the phone. For some properties, they can issue a policy immediately based on the age of the home. If a home was built after 1978, I believe they can just issue a policy; otherwise, they need to do an on-site inspection.

The next item would be to have the property inspected. This can be done in several ways. I typically have someone take a look at the property and fill out an inspection form and then forward the form to me. I have, over the years, created my own home inspection form that is used by me or those that I direct. The document is simple and easy to follow.

You start with the exterior of the home and work your way to the inside. It is what I call a dot sheet where all you do is check off the items with a number system. If you check off number 1, it is because that item is in need of replacement, and if the number checked is a 5, it is in great condition.

Please see the *sample inspection worksheet* I created.

Sample Inspection Worksheet

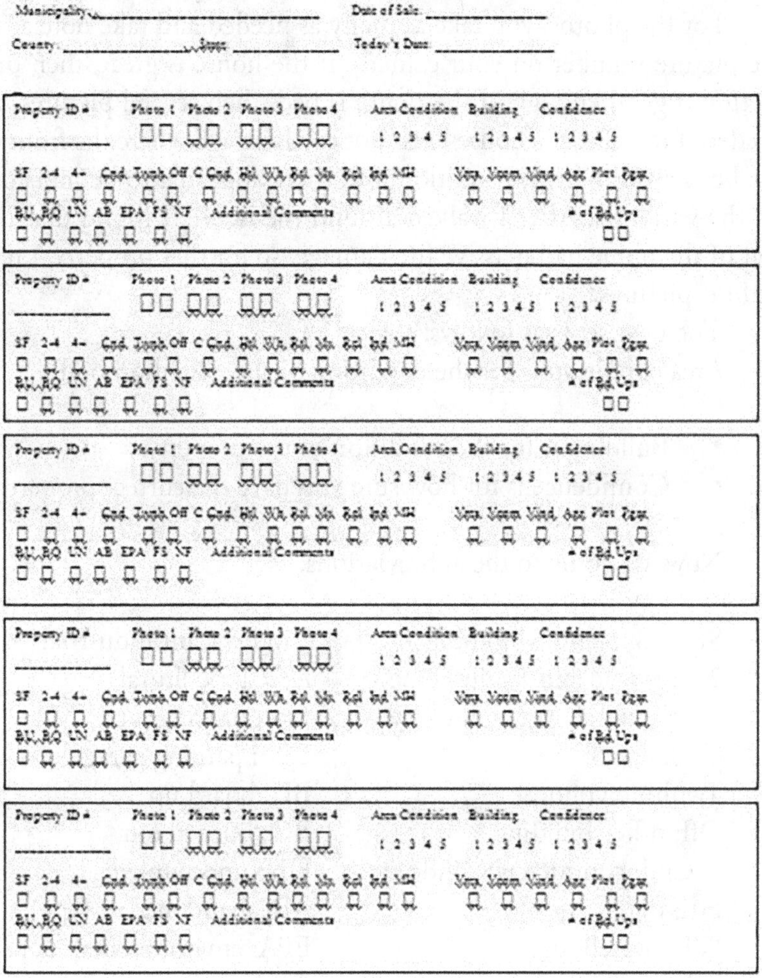

This inspection form can be completed by almost anyone after they have been given the codes. I will go over how to compete the form step by step.

At the top of the page, you fill in the municipality and the date of the sale.

The next line is for the county, state, and the date you looked at the property.

The property ID is the classification given by the tax collector.

For the photos, you take as many as needed and take note as to the picture number on your camera. If the house is great, then one picture is good enough; if the house is bad, then several pictures are needed. I remember a house I saw not too long ago where the front of the house was in great condition, but there appeared to be moisture on the windows. After I walked around the house, I found that the rear of the home had massive fire damage, so for that property, I had all four pictures.

The next set is as follows:

Area condition is for the condition of the neighborhood.

- Building is for the condition of the property.
- Confidence is for how sure you have the correct property.

Now, we come to the abbreviations:

SF: single-family home
2–4: two- to four-family home
4+: five and above family home
Cnd: condo
Twnh: townhouse
Off: office building
C Cnd: commercial condo
Htl: hotel
WH: warehouse
Rtl: retail building
Mx: mixed use
Rel: religious use
Ind: industrial
MH: mobile home
Vres: vacant residential
Vcom: vacant commercial
Vind: vacant industrial
Agr: agricultural
Plot: parking lot
Pgar: parking garage
BU: board up
BO: burned out
UN: unoccupied
AB: abandoned
EPA: environmental
FS: for sale
NF: not found

HOME INSPECTION CHECKLIST

Property Address:_______________________________ Inspection Date: ___________

EXTERIOR 1 2 3 4 5

A. Mailbox - - - - -
B. House / Apt #'s - - - - -
C. Driveway ____________ - - - - -
__ asphalt __ concrete __ sand __ gravel
D. Stairs / Steps
E. Walkway / Sidewalks - - - - -
F. Fence(s) ____________ - - - - -
G. Wall(s) - - - - -
H. Grading to house - - - - -
I. Porch / Patio____________ - - - - -
J. Aluminum Gutter(s) - - - - -
K. Leader / Downspout - - - - -
L. Fascia - - - - -
a. __ painted __ aluminum
M. Soffit(s) - - - - -
a. painted aluminum
N. Trim - - - - -
O. Entry Doors
a. Front :__________ - - - - -
b. Side:__________ - - - - -
c. Rear :__________ - - - - -
P. Door Frames
a. Front :__________ - - - - -
b. Side:__________ - - - - -
c. Rear :__________ - - - - -
Q. Front Door Locks - - - - -
R. Rear / Side Door Locks - - - - -
S. Window(s)__________ - - - - -
Type:__________
Shades/Curtains ______ - - - - -
T. Screens - - - - -
U. Siding __________ - - - - -
V. Framing. - - - - -
W. Roof: years remaining _____ - - - - -
__asphalt __ wood __ tile __ metal
X. Garage / G. Door / Carport - - - - -
____
Swimming Pool_________ - - - - -
Landscaping: - - - - -
Notes:
____
____
____
____
____
____

PLUMBING / LAUNDRY CONNECTION 1 2 3 4 5

1. Water Supply: _________ - - - - -
2. Sewer System: - - - - -
3. Hot Water Unit: _________ - - - - -
4. Washing Machine: - - - - -
5. Dryer: ___ gas ___ elect - - - - -
6. Well system: Y N - - - - -

ELECTRICAL SYSTEM 1 2 3 4 5

1. Main service line _______ - - - - -
2. Capacity: ___ Amps ____ V - - - - -
3. Main disconnect: Y N - - - - -
4. Main ground: __________ - - - - -
5. GFCI: Y N - - - - -
6. Wall Outlets: __________
7. Light Switches: _________ - - - - -
8. Outlet/switch covers - - - - -
9. Service Box:_________ - - - - -
Notes. ____________________________
____

1 2 3 4 5

ATTIC Inspected: __ Yes __ No
1. Roof/ Sheathing - - - - -
2. Ventilation - - - - -
3. Water leaks Yes No

CRAWLSPACE __ Yes __ No
1. Type: __________ - - - - -
2. Framing - - - - -
3. Footings - - - - -

HVAC (Package – Split – Window - Wall) 1 2 3 4 5
1. HVAC Condenser - - - - -
2. HVAC Evaporator - - - - -
3. Ductwork:__________ - - - - -
4. Security Cage - - - - -
5. Main Disconnect exterior
6. A/C grills __________ - - - - -
7. A/C Filter ____x_____ - - - - -
Notes:____________________________
____
____

Step 5: Three Ways to Advertise My Deal

When we get a property, we need to see what we can do to sell the property the quickest. I like to use to online free sites first, and then I will go to eBay before I go to a realtor. If I am going to use the online sites, I first go to the website postlets.com and create a free account.

Postlets free account:

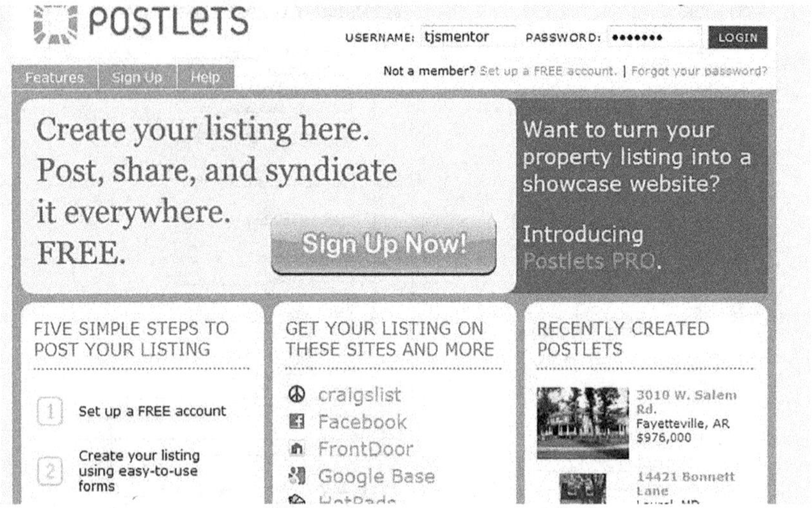

All you need to do is sign up now and create your own free account. From there, you just log in and maintain your files. With this site, you can also link your post on other sites such as craigslist.com, Facebook.com, frontdoor.com, and many more. It is just a matter of getting all the info into the page and let it create the advertisement for you.

Example of my Postlets brochure I placed on Craigslist:

Thomas Senatore | Bayliner Properties | request more info | 239-541-1517

3421 ROCK CREEK DR, Port Charlotte, FL

Gulf Access, investor special, must sell, OBO

Send to Friend

Share Listing

3BR/2BA Single Family House

offered at $60,000

Year Built	1974
Sq Footage	903
Bedrooms	3
Bathrooms	2 full, 0 partial
Floors	1
Parking	Unspecified
Lot Size	10,000 sqft
HOA/Maint	$0 per month

Front View

click on thumbnail to enlarge

DESCRIPTION

Great single family home in quiet neighborhood, ready for a new family, needs a bit of work to be your dream water retreat.

PROPERTY FEATURES

- Tile floor
- Living room
- Yard

COMMUNITY FEATURES

- Covered parking
- Laundry on-site

OTHER SPECIAL FEATURES

- Gulf Access, Boaters dream, don't miss out, will go fast

ADDITIONAL LINKS

- Walk Score: 8
- Local schools
- Mortgage calculator

The next way would be to place the property on eBay and list your property that way. The auction can either be very short or for many days; you choose the time length. Below is the listing where the property shows it was sold for $50,000.

I placed the property on eBay on July 31, and it was sold on August 2, only two days after it was listed. Now, this is not always the case, but I have to say, if you price the property correctly, it will sell fast. I cannot say this enough; if you get greedy and try to hold out for the top dollar, you can lose. If you sell fast and move to the next deal, then you win over and over again. On this property, we had several calls and e-mails from investors wanting additional information. They all had the same comment; they wanted to know if it was a short sale because the price was so low. I had to explain to them that I purchased the property for back taxes and that the debt had been removed. They were getting a property free and clear of all debts with the exception of the tax bill that would be due at the end of the year. Since we pay our taxes in December, the bills have not been sent and payment not due.

A quick note here on this deal. Had I not needed to show this example to a group of investors that I could sell a property in days, I would have made another $10,000 as I have a backup offer of $60,000 for the property. Not that I believe the deal would not close, but I like to take backup offers just in case the buyer backs out.

Step 6: Negotiating the Sale

When we buy and sell from tax liens and tax deeds, the negotiation is so much easier. We are not dealing with sellers, and there are no inspections to be completed before the deal closes.

I have to pay a price for the home somewhere between taxes owed and the current market value. I usually get a price closer to the taxes owed than any other value. When we are dealing with the tax collector, there are no negotiations on the sale of the property; the price they start at is the price. Tax collectors will not lower the open bid below the taxes due unless it is a county-owned property and no one bid at the previous sale.

So then the only negotiating comes from when I sell the property and not when I buy. If I list the property and I have it for well below the actual price but well above the price I paid, I am in control of the deal. If I have to lower my price in order to sell the property, and then that is exactly what I will do. With my property, I spoke to the investor from eBay three times before he placed a bid. He offered me $40,000, and I said no, $50,000 is my minimum, and he would have to pay all my expenses. It was about three minutes later when he purchased the property.

If I were to hold out for a higher amount, I would have been able to profit a bit more money. But if you look at the time invested and the profit made, I did very well. When we have a property that is priced well below market value, it is easy to sell quickly. It is when we get caught up in the profit we might make that we fail to make a profit. Price your deals correctly, and you will sell them all day long; price them too high, and you will carry an inventory.

Step 7: The Closing: Getting Paid

This is by far the easiest part of all the training. I like to use PayPal as well as my merchant account to get paid. If I sell on eBay, they take the money and just send it to my bank account for me. If I have to use my merchant account, the money again goes directly to my bank account. If I have the price too high or the buyer does not feel comfortable, then I need to go to the next level and use a title company to close the deal. A title company will charge much more than eBay would or that of my merchant account. On the merchant account, it is about 3.9¢ per dollar. This can add up, but it is just the cost of doing business.

With a title company, they will do all the paperwork and get all the documents signed, notarized, and filed with the county. All you have to do is give them the instructions as to where the money is to be deposited.

After the property is sold and the deal has closed, the title company will send you a copy of the forms for your records. They will give you the documents needed when you file your income tax return for the following year. When all is said and done, you will have moved several properties and made more money than you can ever have imagined.

What are some of the forms and/or paperwork needed is a question I get asked often. Not to mention the fact that I am told that the title company they spoke to said you cannot sell a tax deeded property.

Let me address the forms and paperwork needed first. You will be required to use several documents when the transfer of real estate is desired, and I will list the most common documents used.

1. *Purchase and sale contract:* This can be found on the Internet, and these are relatively easy to use. If you are having trouble, you can always ask a friend who is a realtor for some help, and I am confident they would help you out. I personally like to look up the standard realtor contract for the state in which I am selling one of my properties and use it as most people there would be familiar with that document.
2. *Property disclosure form:* This document is used for you as the seller to tell the potential buyer any and all known conditions of the property you have knowledge of. Since most

all of my properties were purchased and sold without me being in the property, my disclosure is pretty much states I have no knowledge of any know conditions.

3. *HUD-1/closing statement:* This would be the transaction summary to show how all the proceeds were applied, and this is typically done when using an attorney or a title company to handle the sale of the property.
4. *Title search:* This is used when an attorney or title company handles the closing for you, or the buyer is getting financing to purchase this property. What this report does is list any and all conditions, exclusions, and issues that may be present with the title to this property. Any liens against the property would appear here and would need to be paid before the closing is concluded; otherwise, the new owner could be liable to pay those fees.
5. *Deed:* This is the document that indicates who owns the property. When dealing with a title company, a warranty deed is typically issued, and a title insurance policy goes with it. We like to use the special warranty deed where we only guarantee the quality of title for the period of time we have owned the property. A quit claim deed is also used, and this is where the seller gives no warranty about the clarity of title to the property at all.
6. *Quiet title action:* This is known as the cleaning or clearing of the title when the transfer was due to the sale for back taxes. Some states require that this be completed before the new owner has clear, insurable, and marketable title. It does not mean you cannot sell the property; it just means that it cannot be insured, and there might exist a cloud on title for several years. What this quiet title action does is to inform any and all interested parties that the title was taken from the former owner, and if you feel your interest was not preserved, you have the opportunity to come forward now. If someone did come forward, the investor who purchased the tax deed would not lose out; they would get paid the

amount as if it were redeemed. In some cases, there is an additional interest paid to the investor, and in other cases, there are no additional amounts paid. To quiet a title normally takes five to ten months, and fees start around $600 and go up from there depending on the complexity of the case.

7. *Alternative action:* Although the quiet title action would be the preferred method, there are several companies who will certify the tax deed sale and issue title insurance in a matter of weeks which will allow you to sell the property with a warranty deed and insurable title. The company I use all the time is Clear to Sell located at 501 S. Flagler Drive, Suite 201, West Palm Beach, Florida, 33401. Their website is www.cleartosell.com, and I deal mostly with Dawn. Tell her your one of my referrals and ask for a discount; you never know when you can save some money based on who you know. I can usually get a research outcome letter and tax deed research certificate in less than three weeks which as investor, time is money, and time lost is money lost.

The process is just as easy as I have explained, and the deals go that fast. I challenge you today to go out and do a deal where you get a tax deed and close faster than the five days it took me. On that day, I will look forward to shaking your hand and telling you how impressed I am you took action and exceeded the master.

CHAPTER 7

Four Easy Steps

In this chapter, I will show you the process I have used that has helped me accumulate all that we have today. My system is simple to use, and all that is required is for you to follow the steps I have shared, and you should quickly see your real estate portfolio grow. I have included forms I have found on the Internet to help you along with your process. These forms are readily available to find and can be used by you. I would, however, suggest that you always consult with an attorney before using any forms you get from an outside source.

I have been using these techniques for years, and as each year passes, I find that more of the counties are going to the Internet sales, and it has become easier to buy in this fashion.

I have put together the four easy steps you need to follow to start having success. The results will vary on the individual, but if you put forth the effort, the results are sure to follow.

I have trained many investors, and all have had different results. Some set goals to make a little extra, and others set goals to be financially independent. The goals were set, and the goals were attained. I want you to remember that our success was not a destination, but rather, it was a journey that continues to this day.

Here, I present *four* easy steps for you to follow that will make money using the Internet to buy tax lien certificate's or the tax deed's from the comfort of your home. Use the steps after you have reviewed the entire book. I encourage you to not take shortcuts and not to skip any of the steps provided. I have taken lengths to make this as simple as possible and know you will enjoy reading this series.

Step 1: When

The first step you will need to do is find out when the sales will be held. There are several diffident ways this can be done, and I will outline them for you in this section. We have on our website a *free* listing of the tax sales around the country that you can sign up to view. On this calendar, we provide the following: date of the sale, if it is a tax deed sale or a tax lien sale, number of parcels up for auction, and the price for the sale list if you wanted to purchase this. This is a great resource, and I myself use this on a regular basis. I can see someone getting five to ten of these lists every month and buying tax liens and tax deeds.

Now, after you have located where the sales are, you now can plan which direction you intend in going. You will need to decide if you are going after the sales where they are held in your general location. If so, do you have determined if you have the ability to attend these auctions? Are you looking for only the Internet-type tax lien and tax deed sales? If so, you can review our *free* calendar. To get this information, just go to our website at www.TaxLienAndDeed.com and sign up into our members-only site (free) for the list.

All of the tax sale dates are published by law and can be found in locations around the county where the public has unrestricted access. This would usually be a government building such as a library, post office, city hall, community center, or police station. It is state law that these lists be posted in a public location and must be published in a local newspaper of general circulation for which that tax collector is located.

There are several ways in which you can get these tax sale lists. You need to find a way to get them if you intend on bidding on any properties.

1. The lists can also be requested from the tax collector, and they must make the list available to anyone who requests

one; they cannot deny you this list. Here is the catch: they must make it available, but they do not have to supply it for free.

Many of the tax collectors have these lists available for free such as states like New Jersey. All the tax collectors I have attended their sales have made the list available at least three weeks prior to their sales. They even provide updated lists each day if you request one. The only catch is that they will require that you come in person and get one from the tax collector's counter. I have worked it out where by getting to know the people who make up the tax collectors staff and being nice, they have e-mailed me and faxed me the lists on a regular basis. It is truly amazing what a little kindness can do.

This is an example of a tax lien list.

06/29/09
07:42:17

BOROUGH OF LODI
Tax Sale List

Page

Rpt Selections: Block First to Last
Lot
Qual
Bill board only accounts: N

Sale Date: 06/29/09
Balance Type: Property Tax
Sort Sequence: Blk/Lot

Note: 'CR' - Account has Prior Year Credit
'P' - A Payment has been Posted to Property
'*' - Multiple Balance Total
Costs are Total for Property

Block	Lot(s)	Qual	Owner Name	Property Location		Principal	Interest	Costs	Total
1	2		GATOLLARI,CLIRIM & NIZAMA	161 FARNHAM AVE	T	1,657.00	48.05	34.10	1,739.15
1	4		GATOLLARI,CLIRIM & NIZAMA	163 FARNHAM AVE	T	2,703.09	78.39	55.63	2,837.11
1	35		RANDAZZO,CIRO & ANTONINA	216 HARRISON AVE	T	5,509.86	222.28	100.00	5,832.14
2	11		CATANIA,ROSE(S)	221 FARNHAM AVE	T	6,226.14	360.91	100.00	6,687.05

With the list above from the Lodi, New Jersey, tax collector, you can see that the information is extremely limited. I was at this sale as I try to attend many sales across the country on a regular basis. All the data I had was the lot, block, owner's name, property address, principal amount of taxes owed, interest to date on the taxes, cost of the sale, and the total amount of the lien if purchased today. Everything else that I need, which is also very important, had to be manually researched, and I had to take each property and look them up one by one. The sale list was six pages long and included over eighty properties. With a list of this length, it would take about two to three days to properly research the properties. Research will be covered in the next section. Just know that the research part is probably the most important step in the entire process. Below is a copy of the enhanced list that our company provides and I use regularly.

Lodi, New Jersey, tax lien sale list

1 New Jersey Tax Sale 06/29/09 FIPS# 34003

	Seq	Parcel number	Owner Name	Street Address/Location	Minimum Bid	Size	Value		Use	Loan Amo	Sale Date	La
3												
4	1	1 2	GATOLLARI, CLIRIM & NIZAMA	161 FARNHAM AVE	$1,739.15	50x100	$235,700.00	Homestead	1s-s		6/29/2009	
5	2	1 4	GATOLLARI, CLIRIM & NIZAMA	163 FARNHAM AVE	$2,837.11	50x100	$384,500.00		2s-b		6/29/2009	
6	3	1 35	RANDAZZO, CIRO & ANTONIA	216 HARRISON AVE	$5,832.14						6/29/2009	
7	4	2 11	CATANIA, ROSE (S)	221 FARNHAM AVE	$6,687.05						6/29/2009	
8	5	4 27	ESTEVES, MANUEL	205 WESTMINSTER PL	$3,561.14						6/29/2009	
9	6	5 34	M G & R EQUITIES LLC	152 WESTMINSTER PL	$1,345.42	50x100	$363,700.00	Commercial	2s-f-2ug		6/29/2009	
10	7	6 48	SALAZAR, FAVIO	230 WESTMINSTER PL	$2,909.12						6/29/2009	
11	8	10 39	PATEL, VIRENDRABHAI & KAILASHBE	23 HOME PL	$5,155.48						6/29/2009	
12	9	10 41	RIVERA, JENNY & SANCHEZ, ANTON	27 HOME PL	$4,018.26						6/29/2009	
13	10	10 59	CANNICI, GLEN & EVE JOY	411 PASSAIC AVE	$3,691.56						6/29/2009	
14	11	10 65	GUARINO, BERNARD J (V)	423 PASSAIC AVE	$4,018.21						6/29/2009	
15	12	14 7	ARELLANO, ARIEL & MARGARITA	15 FIRST ST	$5,044.83						6/29/2009	
16	13	17 29 C0006	DANIELS, WALDO	124 HOME PL UNIT 6	$3,371.54						6/29/2009	
17	14	17 29 C0007	124 HOME PL 7 LLC	124 HOME UNIT 7	$2,027.36						6/29/2009	
18	15	19 5	RECON, LLC	430 PASSAIC AVE	$1,999.33	50x216	$274,300.00	Commercial	999		6/29/2009	
19	16	19 9	LAUGHLIN, SUSAN	448 PASSAIC AVE	$1,468.61	12 ac	$202,000.00	Homestead	1s-f		6/29/2009	
20	17	22 6	CARRINO, KAREN	72 CHESTNUT ST	$6,835.76						6/29/2009	
21	18	26 9	RADOJEVIC, DRAGOLJUB	37 CHESTNUT ST	$8,867.88						6/29/2009	
22	19	27 6	ESTUPINAN, ARACELY	98 TERRACE AVE	$12,326.93						6/29/2009	
23	20	27 8.04	RIVERA, ARLEEN	27 NORWOOD AVE	$2,001.83						6/29/2009	
24	21	29 1.01 C005F	VANTERPOOL, SONIA P	44 SO MAIN ST S5F	$1,014.67	condo	$139,700.00	condo		700 sf	6/29/2009	
25	22	29 1.02	FIRST STATES INV. TRS., L.P.	4 HUNTER ST	$18,551.49						6/29/2009	
26	23	30 26	SCALONE,GEORGE	37 TERHUNE AVE	$15,086.07						6/29/2009	
27	24	33 9	MARCHESE, CYNTHIA ANN	22 MCKINLEY AVE	$2,682.59						6/29/2009	

This list above shows the properties in the same order as the tax collector. The list is in Excel, so I am able to manipulate the list to minimize my time and effort when looking. Notice the lines in yellow. These have been sorted, and I was able to choose the prime properties by sorting the column's "minimum bid" and "value." For the minimum bid, I choose the values between $1,000 and $3,000, and for the maximum bid, I choose the value greater than $125,000. I was then able to highlight all these properties, look up the specific info, and then put back into the original order.

I was able to evaluate my research, determine the best offer price, and create my bid book from this sheet. The bid book is nothing but the inventory list from the tax collector or from a third party with your notes about the property and the values of each property which include the CMV (current market value) and your maximum price based on the amount of profit desired.

The cost of investing, buying the list: States like Pennsylvania are notorious for charging for copies, and this includes the tax sales. I found that many of the jurisdictions in Pennsylvania charge about $1 per page which does not sound too bad unless the list you desire is over one hundred pages long. The lists for the Florida tax sales are typically three hundred to four hundred pages long. Multiply that by $1 per page, and you're looking at about $300–$400 dollars to just see what is for sale and not buy anything at this point. This will easily cut into your profits if your budget is limited.

2. They can be found in the newspaper three to four weeks prior to the auctions.

The lists are always found in the paper, but try to find the paper and try to get it on the day it will be listed. These lists will only be in the newspaper one day per week for three to four consecutive weeks. You will need to go to the area where these papers are sold and buy one. I was able to get a few of these papers and picked up the papers for two Florida tax lien sales. I was able to obtain the Collier County tax sale list newspaper and the Lee County tax sale list newspaper. Below, I have attached several copies from each paper for your reference. Note that there is much to be gained from this type of list as well as much that is lacking.

Here is the front page of the Collier County Paper, the *Naples Daily News.*

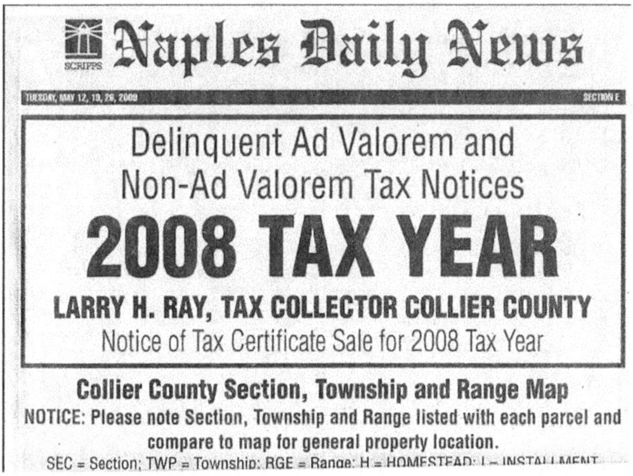

SCRIPPS

Naples Daily News

TUESDAY, MAY 12, 19, 26, 2009 SECTION E

Delinquent Ad Valorem and
Non-Ad Valorem Tax Notices

2008 TAX YEAR

LARRY H. RAY, TAX COLLECTOR COLLIER COUNTY

Notice of Tax Certificate Sale for 2008 Tax Year

Collier County Section, Township and Range Map

NOTICE: Please note Section, Township and Range listed with each parcel and compare to map for general property location.

SEC = Section; TWP = Township; RGE = Range; H = HOMESTEAD; I = INSTALLMENT

Notice how the paper has an entire section dedicated to this sale. The details of the sale were located on the second page of this advertisement.

The taxing authority is required to post the notice of the sale just like the county did in the photo above.

The rules require that the list be published and made available, and the tax collector typically would use the local newspaper and have copies available upon request.

I do not know of any community that would not have a copy on the premises where you could review the paper.

Many try to have several copies for individuals upon request.

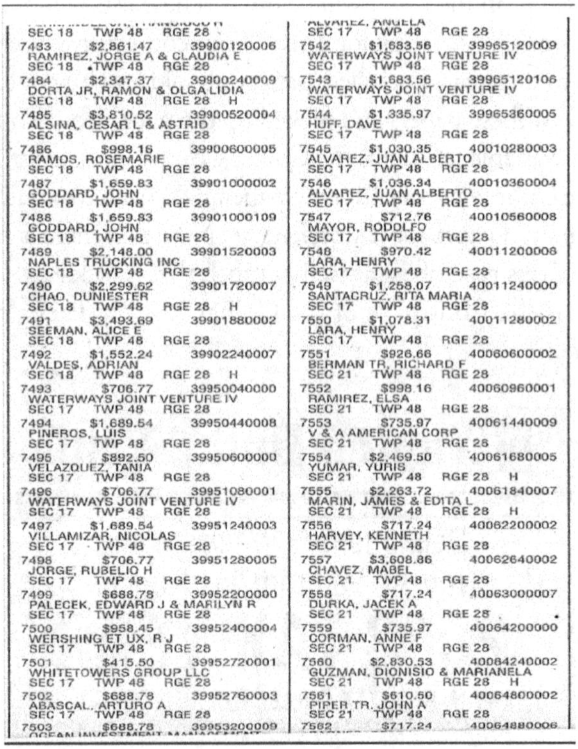
SEC 18 TWP 48 RGE 28
7483 $2,861.47 39900120006
RAMIREZ, JORGE A & CLAUDIA E
SEC 18 TWP 48 RGE 28
7484 $2,347.37 39900240009
DORTA JR, RAMON & OLGA LIDIA
SEC 18 TWP 48 RGE 28 H
7485 $3,810.52 39900520004
ALSINA, CESAR L & ASTRID
SEC 18 TWP 48 RGE 28
7486 $998.16 39900600005
RAMOS, ROSEMARIE
SEC 18 TWP 48 RGE 28
7487 $1,659.83 39901000002
GODDARD, JOHN
SEC 18 TWP 48 RGE 28
7488 $1,659.83 39901000109
GODDARD, JOHN
SEC 18 TWP 48 RGE 28
7489 $2,148.00 39901520003
NAPLES TRUCKING INC
SEC 18 TWP 48 RGE 28
7490 $2,299.62 39901720007
CHAO, DUNIESTER
SEC 18 TWP 48 RGE 28 H
7491 $3,493.69 39901880002
SEEMAN, ALICE E
SEC 18 TWP 48 RGE 28
7492 $1,552.24 39902240007
VALDES, ADRIAN
SEC 18 TWP 48 RGE 28 H
7493 $706.77 39950040000
WATERWAYS JOINT VENTURE IV
SEC 17 TWP 48 RGE 28
7494 $1,689.54 39950440008
PINEROS, LUIS
SEC 17 TWP 48 RGE 28
7495 $892.50 39950600000
VELAZQUEZ, TANIA
SEC 17 TWP 48 RGE 28
7496 $706.77 39951080001
WATERWAYS JOINT VENTURE IV
SEC 17 TWP 48 RGE 28
7497 $1,689.54 39951240003
VILLAMIZAR, NICOLAS
SEC 17 TWP 48 RGE 28
7498 $706.77 39951280005
JORGE, RUBELIO H
SEC 17 TWP 48 RGE 28
7499 $688.78 39952200000
PALECEK, EDWARD J & MARILYN R
SEC 17 TWP 48 RGE 28
7500 $958.45 39952400004
WERSHING ET UX, R J
SEC 17 TWP 48 RGE 28
7501 $415.50 39952720001
WHITETOWERS GROUP LLC
SEC 17 TWP 48 RGE 28
7502 $688.78 39952760003
ABASCAL, ARTURO A
SEC 17 TWP 48 RGE 28
7503 $688.78 39953200009

SEC 17 TWP 48 RGE 28
7542 $1,683.56 39965120009
WATERWAYS JOINT VENTURE IV
SEC 17 TWP 48 RGE 28
7543 $1,683.56 39965120106
WATERWAYS JOINT VENTURE IV
SEC 17 TWP 48 RGE 28
7544 $1,335.97 39965360005
HUFF, DAVE
SEC 17 TWP 48 RGE 28
7545 $1,030.35 40010280003
ALVAREZ, JUAN ALBERTO
SEC 17 TWP 48 RGE 28
7546 $1,036.34 40010360004
ALVAREZ, JUAN ALBERTO
SEC 17 TWP 48 RGE 28
7547 $712.76 40010560008
MAYOR, RODOLFO
SEC 17 TWP 48 RGE 28
7548 $970.42 40011200008
LARA, HENRY
SEC 17 TWP 48 RGE 28
7549 $1,258.07 40011240000
SANTACRUZ, RITA MARIA
SEC 17 TWP 48 RGE 28
7550 $1,078.31 40011280002
LARA, HENRY
SEC 17 TWP 48 RGE 28
7551 $926.66 40060600002
BERMAN TR, RICHARD F
SEC 21 TWP 48 RGE 28
7552 $998.16 40060960001
RAMIREZ, ELSA
SEC 21 TWP 48 RGE 28
7553 $735.97 40061440009
V & A AMERICAN CORP
SEC 21 TWP 48 RGE 28
7554 $2,469.50 40061680005
YUMAR, YURIS
SEC 21 TWP 48 RGE 28 H
7555 $2,263.72 40061840007
MARIN, JAMES & EDITA L
SEC 21 TWP 48 RGE 28 H
7556 $717.24 40062200002
HARVEY, KENNETH
SEC 21 TWP 48 RGE 28
7557 $3,608.86 40062640002
CHAVEZ, MABEL
SEC 21 TWP 48 RGE 28
7558 $717.24 40063000007
DURKA, JACEK A
SEC 21 TWP 48 RGE 28
7559 $735.97 40064200000
CORMAN, ANNE F
SEC 21 TWP 48 RGE 28
7560 $2,830.53 40064240002
GUZMAN, DIONISIO & MARIANELA
SEC 21 TWP 48 RGE 28 H
7561 $610.50 40064800002
PIPER TR, JOHN A
SEC 21 TWP 48 RGE 28
7562 $717.24 40064880006

In the above section of the newspaper from the Collier County, Florida, tax lien certificate sale, the tax liens are listed in item order. If we look at the property listed at the bottom left hand corner of this page, we shall see the following information. The property listed is sale item number 7502; the taxes owed are $688.78 dollars and an eleven-digit property ID number; the property owners are Arturo A. Abascal, and the partial legal description is SEC 17 (section #17), TWP 48 (township #48), and RGE 28 (range #28).

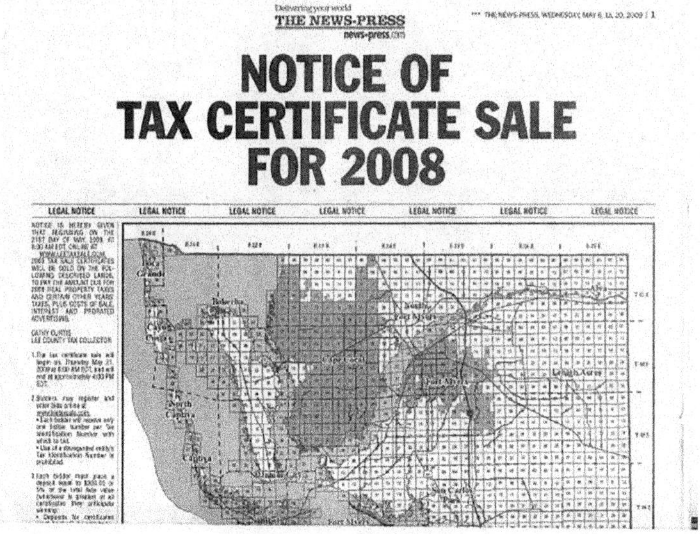
THE NEWS-PRESS

news-press.com

NOTICE OF TAX CERTIFICATE SALE FOR 2008

Above is a copy of the front page of the Lee County newspaper which is referred to as *The New Press*. Again, notice that an entire section of *The New Press* newspaper has been dedicated to this sale. On the next page, you will see what the content of this advertisement has to offer.

68 | THE NEWS-PRESS, WEDNESDAY, MAY 6, 13, 20, 2009

LEGAL NOTICE | LEGAL NOTICE | LEGAL NOTICE | LEGAL NOTICE | LEGAL NOTICE | LEGAL NOTICE | LEGAL NOTICE

This newspaper had the advertisement running for three consecutive weeks prior to the sale. Although the print on the page has been enlarged for the purpose of this booklet, the print is still very small. This is how several investors would build their bid book from and use this paper at the sale.

Each of the above newspapers represents what it is like to obtain the information for the tax lien certificate sales around the country. Each paper had multiple sections with many pages per section. The papers only were distributed on a certain day of the week for three to four weeks prior to the sale. If you did not get the paper at the newspaper stand, you occasionally can get the insert tax sale list from the tax collector. This is only typical in Florida and varies from state to state.

In going over these newspapers, I was overwhelmed with the desire for more information in order to properly research these properties before I felt comfortable to bid. At the sales, I saw many individuals with these newspapers that they appear to have been read and reread many times over, and they were looking very distressed. Had I used that method, I would have had similar results as they did and not have left the sale with almost two hundred tax liens?

3. Some tax collectors maintain websites which can include the current tax sale lists.

As I have traveled across the country, I found that many of the states have moved into the twentieth century and placed much of the information on the Internet. States like Texas, Florida, Arizona, and Colorado, to name a few, have fairly good websites for information when it comes to the tax sales.

I found that the tax deed sales listed in Harris County covers the area in and around Houston, Texas. Most of the counties use one of the two law firms to process the tax deed sales. Harris County is one of the more desirable auctions as the economy around that area typically does well. I have attended their sales often and have yet to see a decline in the number of investors attending the sales nor have I seen a true drop in the values for properties being bid as well.

Property Information

Precinct Number	Sale Date (Sale Nbr)	Cause Number	District Court
1	08/04/2009 (1)	2005-03684	295

Account Number	Judgement Date	Order Issue Date
0211380760009	04/16/2009	06/23/2009

Case Style
HARRIS COUNTY, ET AL VS MCKAY TRUST COMPANY, ET AL

Legal Description
LT 9 BLK 76 INDEPENDENCE HEIGHTS PARK

Physical Address
0 E 40TH ST 77022

Adjudged Value	Estimated Minimum Bid	Status
$16,000	$9,924.72	

Precinct Number	Sale Date (Sale Nbr)	Cause Number	District Court
6	08/04/2009 (1)	2005-09757	61

Account Number	Judgement Date	Order Issue Date
0511770060001	10/26/2006	03/23/2009

Case Style
HARRIS COUNTY, ET AL VS LAURLESE BOYD JR, ET AL

Legal Description
LTS 1 2 & 3 BLK 6 OLEANDER HEIGHTS

Physical Address
4421 EDMUND ST 77020

Adjudged Value	Estimated Minimum Bid	Status
$43,609	$5,456.31	

Precinct Number	Sale Date (Sale Nbr)	Cause Number	District Court
7	08/04/2009 (1)	2002-38427	129

The list above is the actual sale list taken off of the Internet. I first went into the Harris County Texas tax collector's website. From there, I went the tax sale procedures tab found on the left side of the page. Then I went to the bottom of the page and clicked on the link for one of the attorneys that handle the foreclosures for the county.

Linebarger Goggan Blair and Sampson, LLP, are the attorneys that prepare the legal work, and here is the link I went to in order to get the list.

From the information listed, I found there to be over seventy-five pages of properties listed for that month with prices that most investors can afford. The sheets can be sorted by precinct which is how the sales are called off. I can separate the lists and have files made for each of the eight precincts as a constable for each individual precinct calls off his or her listed properties for their area of the county. I then can take this information directly to create a bid book and get all the research completed and complied in one place. With any lists, you will need to understand how the sale works, how the properties are listed, and if there are any differences between counties. I found that this sale is unique in that it is not completely held on the courthouse steps as do most counties in Texas. This sale is conducted in and around a building across from the county building which is located downtown, and to hold this sale at the entrance of this building would make the sale process difficult. This sale is called off by precincts and the constable for each of their respective precincts calls off the auction. This sale is unique as all the constables call off their sales within feet from each other, and they crowd all the bidders in and around this location. This creates some confusion, and many bidders get frustrated and leave which allows us to get more deals.

An example of a Florida sale calendar

<< June   July 2009   August> >

Sun	Mon	Tue	Wed	Thu	Fri	Sat
			1 Auctions 0 Tax Deed 13 Foreclosures 11:00 AM ET	2 Auctions 0 Tax Deed 12 Foreclosures 11:00 AM ET	3	4
5	6 Auctions 0 Tax Deed 16 Foreclosures 11:00 AM ET	7 Auctions 20 Tax Deed 0 Foreclosures 09:00 AM ET	8 Auctions 0 Tax Deed 13 Foreclosures 11:00 AM ET	9 Auctions 0 Tax Deed 4 Foreclosures 11:00 AM ET	10 Auctions 0 Tax Deed 4 Foreclosures 11:00 AM ET	11
12	13 Auctions 0 Tax Deed 15 Foreclosures 11:00 AM ET	14 Auctions 43 Tax Deed 1 Foreclosures 09:00 AM ET	15 Auctions 0 Tax Deed 17 Foreclosures 11:00 AM ET	16 Auctions 0 Tax Deed 16 Foreclosures 11:00 AM ET	17 Auctions 0 Tax Deed 16 Foreclosures 11:00 AM ET	18
19	20 Auctions 0 Tax Deed 22 Foreclosures 11:00 AM ET	21 Auctions 41 Tax Deed 0 Foreclosures 09:00 AM ET	22 Auctions 0 Tax Deed 26 Foreclosures 11:00 AM ET	23 Auctions 0 Tax Deed 24 Foreclosures 11:00 AM ET	24 Auctions 0 Tax Deed 26 Foreclosures 11:00 AM ET	25
26	27 Auctions	28 Auctions	29 Auctions	30 Auctions	31 Auctions	

The list on the preceding page was taken from a Florida online tax deed sale and has all the required information needed to get the research process started. I can pick the type of sale I wish to bid at; it can be either the tax deed or the mortgage foreclosure sale. I can see what amount of inventory will be offered for sale, the time of the sale, as well as the date. If I click on the link for any specific date, I will get the list for that sale. See the list below for a tax deed sale.

I like the state of Florida as I find that much of the desired information can be obtained easily from the websites that offer the sale lists as well as the different county agencies I need to research.

Notice that the information provided here from this county website is much different from that of the other counties that were shown prior.

Here is an example of an auction website that offers many conveniences as shown earlier. I can see from the information provided the date of the auction as well as the type of auction. They list the tax deed case number, the opening bid amount required, the parcel ID as well as the property address, the assessed value, and, lastly, what my bid amount is. From this screen, I can check the information on this property by clicking the links on the bid page. I can go to the tax collector's site to see the tax payment history as well as the amount of taxes for the past.

Bidders Page

Here is the bidder's page, and we can see on the bottom of the page there are hyperlinks to the different sources you will need to make an educated bid offer.

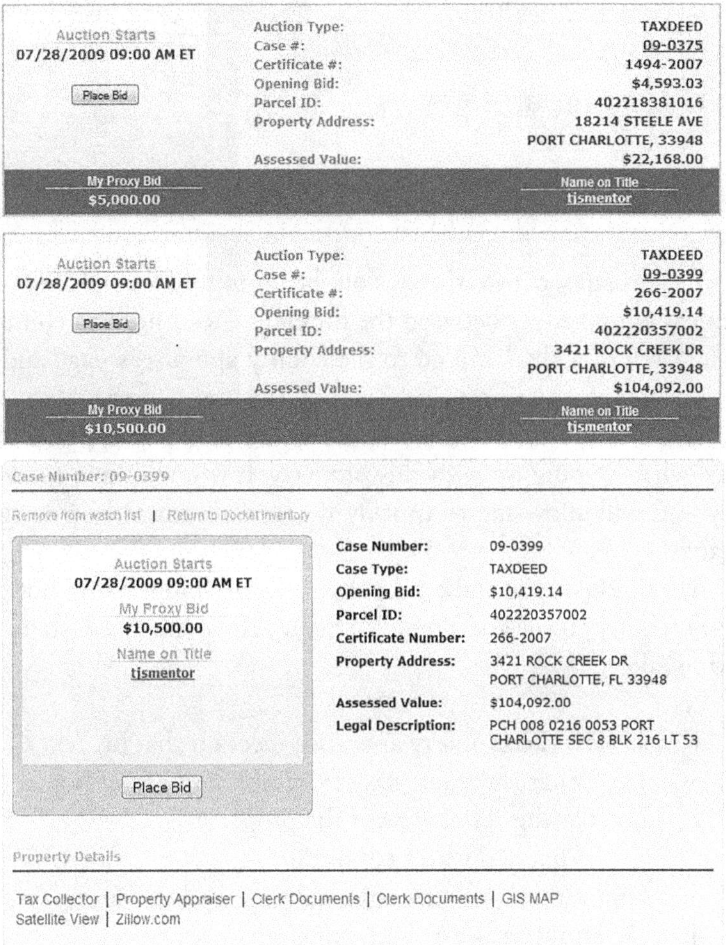

Auction Starts
07/28/2009 09:00 AM ET
Place Bid

Auction Type:	TAXDEED
Case #:	09-0375
Certificate #:	1494-2007
Opening Bid:	$4,593.03
Parcel ID:	402218381016
Property Address:	18214 STEELE AVE PORT CHARLOTTE, 33948
Assessed Value:	$22,168.00

My Proxy Bid $5,000.00 — Name on Title tjsmentor

Auction Starts
07/28/2009 09:00 AM ET
Place Bid

Auction Type:	TAXDEED
Case #:	09-0399
Certificate #:	266-2007
Opening Bid:	$10,419.14
Parcel ID:	402220357002
Property Address:	3421 ROCK CREEK DR PORT CHARLOTTE, 33948
Assessed Value:	$104,092.00

My Proxy Bid $10,500.00 — Name on Title tjsmentor

Case Number: 09-0399

Remove from watch list | Return to Docket Inventory

Auction Starts
07/28/2009 09:00 AM ET
My Proxy Bid
$10,500.00
Name on Title
tjsmentor
Place Bid

Case Number:	09-0399
Case Type:	TAXDEED
Opening Bid:	$10,419.14
Parcel ID:	402220357002
Certificate Number:	266-2007
Property Address:	3421 ROCK CREEK DR PORT CHARLOTTE, FL 33948
Assessed Value:	$104,092.00
Legal Description:	PCH 008 0216 0053 PORT CHARLOTTE SEC 8 BLK 216 LT 53

Property Details

Tax Collector | Property Appraiser | Clerk Documents | Clerk Documents | GIS MAP
Satellite View | Zillow.com

County Appraiser Page

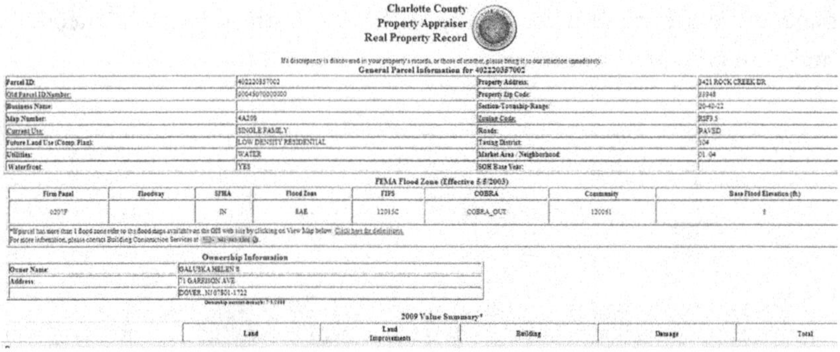

Charlotte County
Property Appraiser
Real Property Record

General Parcel Information for 402220357002

Parcel ID:	402220357002	Property Address:	3421 ROCK CREEK DR
Old Parcel ID Number:	00045070000000	Property Zip Code:	33948
Business Name:		Section-Township-Range:	20-40-22
Map Number:	4A209	Zoning Code:	RSF3.5
Current Use:	SINGLE FAMILY	Roads:	PAVED
Future Land Use (Comp. Plan):	LOW DENSITY RESIDENTIAL	Taxing District:	304
Utilities:	WATER	Market Area / Neighborhood:	01 04
Waterfront:	YES	SOH Base Year:	

FEMA Flood Zone (Effective 5/5/2003)

Firm Panel	Floodway	SFHA	Flood Zone	FIPS	COBRA	Community	Base Flood Elevation (ft.)
0207F		IN	AE	12015C	COBRA_OUT	120061	8

Ownership Information

Owner Name:	GALUSKA HELEN S
Address:	71 GARRISON AVE
	DOVER, NJ 07801-1722

2009 Value Summary*

Land	Land Improvements	Building	Damage	Total

As you can see from the tabs on the bottom of the bidding page, I can easily maneuver between the different sites I need to complete my research quickly. I can go to the county appraiser's page and get much more information as indicated by the photo above.

If I like the property, I will go to the property appraiser first to see what is going on with this property. It will tell me a complete story and will allow me to quickly decide if I will bid or do more research.

When looking at these properties via the Internet and not having the ability to see the home firsthand, there are a few steps you need to take.

1. Review the property appraiser sheet on that property.
    a. What is the lot size, house size, and age of home?
2. Look at the aerial view of the property.
    a. What is the area condition?
3. Find out the current home sales in the last thirty days.
4. Determine at least three exit strategies
    a. Flip, retail, or rental

GIS of the Property

As seen from the image taken from the GIS (geographic information system) mapping program, this property is located in a very desirable waterfront neighborhood. Should I get this property, I am confident that I will have no problem implementing one of my exit strategies of flipping quickly, renting/lease optioning, or selling after rehab.

4. Another way would be to buy the tax sale book or CD from the tax collector directly. California is one of the states that have a book offered prior to the auction that you can purchase. Los Angeles County is also one of the largest counties for listed tax-delinquent properties. This past year, the list was well over three hundred pages, and there probably were close to thirty properties listed per page.

This booklet of information provided from the Los Angeles County tax collector in this book is very informative, and this book is what you will use when you bid at this sale. The sales of the properties are sold in the order they appear in this book, and you can see from the number of delinquent properties that this sale does take several days. The sales start and then continue each day during normal business hours till every parcel has been sold or struck off to the county.

ITEM NO	NSB#	LEGAL DESC / CURRENT ASSESSEE / LOCATION	MIN BID.	IMPS	MB PG PCL CURRENT PARCEL / PRIOR PARCEL
1072	522	TRACT , 13501 LOT 11 ASSESSED TO SOURY,MICKEY LOCATION COUNTY OF LOS ANGELES PROPERTY ADDRESS: VAC/ELIZABETH LK/VIC LOOKABOUT R ELIZABETH LK CA93532	$1,728		3224 005 006 04/3224 005 006
1073	522	TRACT # 15821 LOT 2 ASSESSED TO DEPUY,MARJORIE ET AL PERRY,JOHN M JR LOCATION COUNTY OF LOS ANGELES PROPERTY ADDRESS: VAC/ELIZABETH LK/VIC HUNGRYJACK ELIZABETH LK CA93532	$2,285		3224 008 002 04/3224 008 002
1074	522	TRACT # 12787 LOT 37 ASSESSED TO JONES,ROCKY D LOCATION COUNTY OF LOS ANGELES PROPERTY ADDRESS: VAC/LITTLEBOY DR/VIC WALKATOP RD ELIZABETH LK CA93532	$2,145		3224 011 014 04/3224 011 014
1075	522	TRACT # 17326 LOT 145 ASSESSED TO BISSON,SCOTT LOCATION COUNTY OF LOS ANGELES PROPERTY ADDRESS: VAC/SANDROCK DR/VIC RANCH CLUB ELIZABETH LK CA93532	$2,697		3224 022 017 02/3224 022 017
1077	522	TRACT # 24829 LOT 17 ASSESSED TO NIVEN,MARY E LOCATION COUNTY OF LOS ANGELES PROPERTY ADDRESS: VAC/COR RANCH CLUB/MONTELLO DR ELIZABETH LK CA93532	$1,621		3224 023 027 04/3224 023 027
1081	522	TRACT # 15076 LOT 7 ASSESSED TO MARTIN,WILLIAM C LOCATION COUNTY OF LOS ANGELES PROPERTY ADDRESS: VAC/BOXTREE RD/VIC BROOKWOOD RD ELIZABETH LAKE CA93532	$2,721		3225 003 007 04/3225 003 007

On the prior page is a section of the Los Angeles, California, tax deed book that was purchased for less the $35. The information provided here is much better than attempting to use the newspaper based again on the number of properties listed up for auction.

5. The last way is to go to a third party that has gathered all the sale information and offers it back up for sale.

We offer a competitively priced list of tax sales with enhanced details of the properties listed for sale. These lists are a cumulative effort of many people from across the country to ensure the most comprehensive list of the sales. You can purchase these lists on our website, www.taxlienanddeed.com, and have these downloaded directly to your computer in Excel format. This is to your advantage as you can sort, manipulate, and add columns as needed to help you create your own bid books. I used our lists to create my bid book for the Collier County, Florida, tax lien certificate sale. The sale originally had over 27,000 parcels, and they were all listed in the newspaper which was shown previously. As you will see, our list is user-friendly and very easy to manipulate and sort as needed to enhance the means in which you can interpret the information.

In our website, we have provided the investor with this tool to minimize the cost of the information needed to bid at the auctions. Similar services have been offered by competing firms at prices monthly from $50 to $200 for similar lists. Our lists can be purchased with our annual membership which would entitle you to obtain three hundred lists for the twelve-month period. These enhanced lists would normally cost $10–$30 each but with our offer cost less than $3 per list. Please visit our website at www.TaxLienAndDeed.com for the pricing for our members. Our membership to our site is free!

Enhanced Tax Sale List

1	Seq #	Street Address/Location	Town	Minimum Bi Total	Legal	Land	Improvement	Total	Property Address
1630	1629	57307 TAMIAMI TRL E	NAPLES	$295.97	NON-AG ACREAGE	$19,900.00	$0.00	$19,900.00	57307 TAMIAMI TRL E
1631	1630	57070 TAMIAMI TRL E	NAPLES	$985.33	SINGLE FAMILY	$8,410.00	$58,733.00	$67,143.00	57070 TAMIAMI TRL E
1632	1631	421 12TH AVE S	NAPLES	$2,285.99	CONDOMINIUM	$0.00	$207,139.00	$207,139.00	421 12TH AVE S
1633	1632	4031 GULF SHORE BLVD N	NAPLES	$6,814.80	CONDOMINIUM	$0.00	$618,517.00	$618,517.00	4031 GULF SHORE BLVD N
1634	1633	4031 GULF SHORE BLVD N	NAPLES	$7,255.18	CONDOMINIUM	$0.00	$658,517.00	$668,517.00	4031 GULF SHORE BLVD N
1635	1634	4031 GULF SHORE BLVD N	NAPLES	$7,519.38	CONDOMINIUM	$0.00	$682,517.00	$662,517.00	4031 GULF SHORE BLVD N
1636	1635	1910 GULF SHORE BLVD N	NAPLES	$776.07	CONDOMINIUM	$0.00	$278,721.00	$107,805.00	1910 GULF SHORE BLVD N
1637	1636	1910 GULF SHORE BLVD N	NAPLES	$4,324.88	CONDOMINIUM	$0.00	$391,499.00	$391,499.00	1910 GULF SHORE BLVD N
1638	1637	310 14TH AVE S	NAPLES	$776.25	CONDOMINIUM	$0.00	$70,000.00	$70,000.00	310 14TH AVE S
1639	1638	475 15TH AVE S	NAPLES	$4,868.03	SINGLE FAMILY	$1,662,500.00	$205,567.00	$479,626.00	475 15TH AVE S
1640	1639	696 15TH AVE S	NAPLES	$24,529.01	SINGLE FAMILY	$2,065,500.00	$162,096.00	$2,227,596.00	696 15TH AVE S
1641	1640	460 15TH AVE S	NAPLES	$34,000.71	SINGLE FAMILY	$1,715,000.00	$1,372,963.00	$3,087,963.00	460 15TH AVE S
1642	1641	440 15TH AVE S	NAPLES	$21,893.46	SINGLE FAMILY	$1,715,000.00	$273,195.00	$1,988,195.00	440 15TH AVE S
1643	1642	414 15TH AVE S	NAPLES	$20,883.04	SINGLE FAMILY	$1,741,250.00	$155,162.00	$1,896,412.00	414 15TH AVE S
1644	1643	656 16TH AVE S	NAPLES	$11,832.82	SINGLE FAMILY	$1,715,000.00	$1,144,970.00	$1,112,275.00	656 16TH AVE S
1645	1644	980 AQUA CIR	NAPLES	$36,518.90	MISCELLANEOUS	$3,267,000.00	$49,702.00	$3,316,702.00	980 AQUA CIR
1646	1645	1713 4TH ST S	NAPLES	$18,972.37	MISCELLANEOUS	$1,715,000.00	$7,855.00	$1,722,855.00	1713 4TH ST S
1647	1646	711 18TH AVE S	NAPLES	$19,145.20	MISCELLANEOUS	$1,715,000.00	$23,554.00	$1,738,554.00	711 18TH AVE S
1648	1647	953 18TH AVE S	NAPLES	$43,031.92	SINGLE FAMILY	$3,024,000.00	$1,753,341.00	$3,946,259.00	953 18TH AVE S
1649	1648	1750 4TH ST S	NAPLES	$33,968.48	SINGLE FAMILY	$1,767,500.00	$1,355,478.00	$3,122,978.00	1750 4TH ST S
1650	1649	1600 4TH ST S	NAPLES	$19,776.93	MISCELLANEOUS	$1,767,500.00	$28,439.00	$1,795,939.00	1600 4TH ST S
1651	1650	1756 3RD ST S	NAPLES	$17,635.51	SINGLE FAMILY	$1,479,000.00	$122,420.00	$1,601,420.00	1756 3RD ST S
1652	1651	1990 4TH ST S	NAPLES	$4,825.18	SINGLE FAMILY	$2,250,000.00	$229,029.00	$1,809,075.00	1990 4TH ST S
1653	1652	2000 5TH ST S	NAPLES	$13,691.94	SINGLE FAMILY	$1,851,792.00	$152,578.00	$1,281,148.00	2000 5TH ST S
1654	1653	1940 6TH ST S	NAPLES	$25,856.48	SINGLE FAMILY	$2,185,400.00	$162,777.00	$2,348,177.00	1940 6TH ST S
1655	1654	688 21ST AVE S	NAPLES	$23,480.27	SINGLE FAMILY	$1,782,000.00	$350,332.00	$2,132,332.00	688 21ST AVE S

As seen on this list, the information can be sorted, and there is a section for your bid data as needed. I can sort by any column listed above and pick and highlight as needed.

Step 2: What

The second step you need to learn is how to know the items that are listed for sale are. They could be land, mobile homes, single-family homes and multifamily homes, or commercial and agricultural properties. Once you determine the type of property, then you can work on your strategy.

Land: Raw land is usually a good safe bet in most economic times. It is commonly referred to as *land banking*. As I look over the lists of properties up for sale in Florida, I find that much of the inventory for sale is vacant residential land as indicated by the use code from the county.

I will need to look up this property, and by using the Internet sites like Google, MapQuest, and others, I can get a good sense of what the area surrounding the property is like. If I find a vacant lot that is partially cleared and is sandwiched between two very nice homes, then that is a property I would like to buy.

But on the other hand, if the property is overgrown and is in a neighborhood of all vacant lots, then I would pass. As we look at these properties, I have to determine which ones are good and which ones are bad.

Here is an example of a good vacant lot:

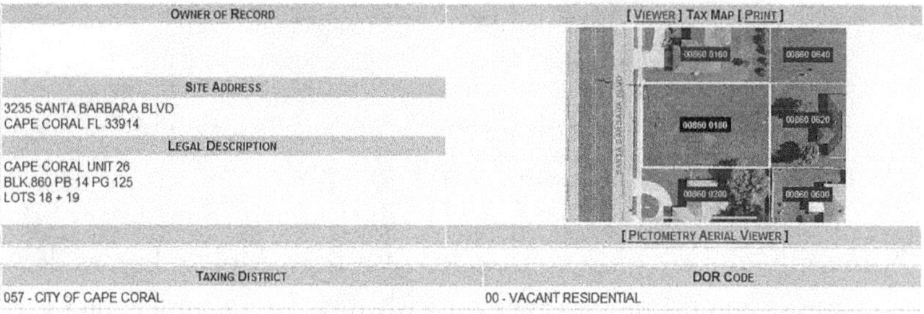
OWNER OF RECORD

SITE ADDRESS
3235 SANTA BARBARA BLVD
CAPE CORAL FL 33914

LEGAL DESCRIPTION
CAPE CORAL UNIT 26
BLK.860 PB 14 PG 125
LOTS 18 + 19

[VIEWER] TAX MAP [PRINT]

[PICTOMETRY AERIAL VIEWER]

TAXING DISTRICT	DOR CODE
057 - CITY OF CAPE CORAL	00 - VACANT RESIDENTIAL

Notice that this lot is cleared and next to houses on all sides. This lot is highly marketable and can be sold quickly to another investor or homeowner.

Here is an example of an average valued lot.

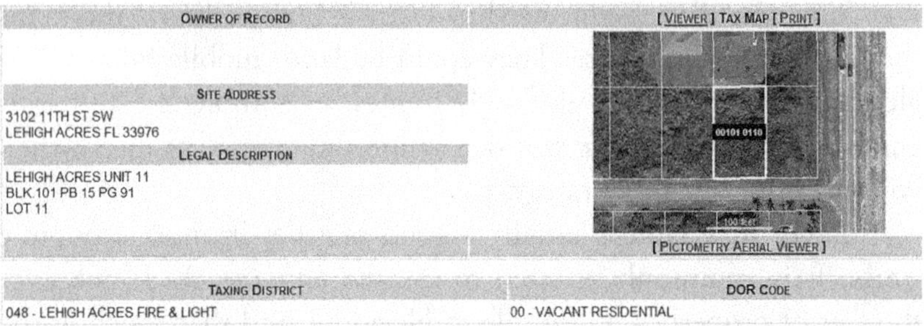
OWNER OF RECORD

[VIEWER] TAX MAP [PRINT]

SITE ADDRESS

3102 11TH ST SW
LEHIGH ACRES FL 33976

LEGAL DESCRIPTION

LEHIGH ACRES UNIT 11
BLK 101 PB 15 PG 91
LOT 11

[PICTOMETRY AERIAL VIEWER]

TAXING DISTRICT	DOR CODE
048 - LEHIGH ACRES FIRE & LIGHT	00 - VACANT RESIDENTIAL

Notice that this lot is not cleared, and the only house is to the rear.

This lot is marketable and can be sold to another investor or homeowner with limited profit.

Here is an example of a less desirable lot:

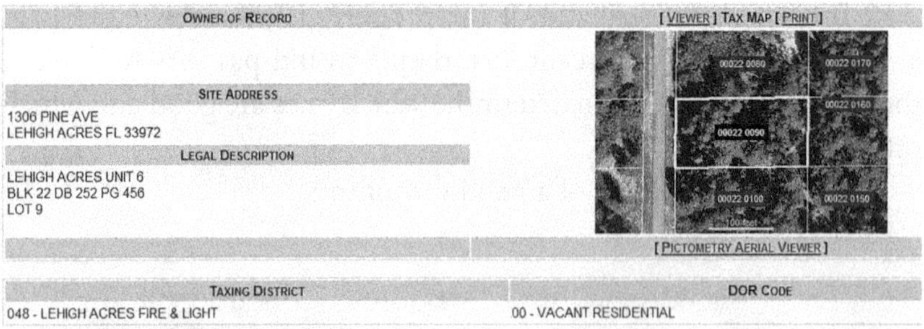
OWNER OF RECORD

[VIEWER] TAX MAP [PRINT]

SITE ADDRESS

1306 PINE AVE
LEHIGH ACRES FL 33972

LEGAL DESCRIPTION

LEHIGH ACRES UNIT 6
BLK 22 DB 252 PG 456
LOT 9

[PICTOMETRY AERIAL VIEWER]

TAXING DISTRICT	DOR CODE
048 - LEHIGH ACRES FIRE & LIGHT	00 - VACANT RESIDENTIAL

Notice that this lot is overgrown as are all the lots. This lot is not very marketable and could not be sold quickly.

Mobile homes: They are found in the lower-income areas of the community and are great sources for cash flow. Mobile homes draw little attention and have very good cash flow based on the fact that they can be purchased for such low dollar amounts. These properties can be purchased for under $20,000 and can be rented out weekly for about $150 per week. With income at that level, you would collect about $7,800 per year, and in three years, your investment would have netted you a 100% return.

Here is an example of a mobile home property:

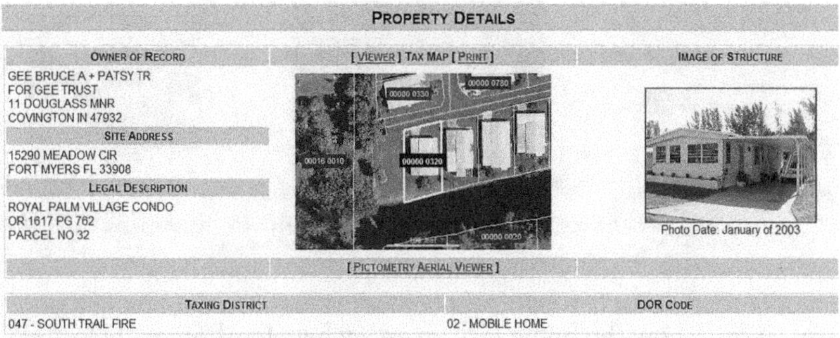
PROPERTY DETAILS

OWNER OF RECORD
GEE BRUCE A + PATSY TR
FOR GEE TRUST
11 DOUGLASS MNR
COVINGTON IN 47932

SITE ADDRESS
15290 MEADOW CIR
FORT MYERS FL 33908

LEGAL DESCRIPTION
ROYAL PALM VILLAGE CONDO
OR 1617 PG 762
PARCEL NO 32

[VIEWER] TAX MAP [PRINT]

IMAGE OF STRUCTURE
Photo Date: January of 2003

[PICTOMETRY AERIAL VIEWER]

TAXING DISTRICT	DOR CODE
047 - SOUTH TRAIL FIRE	02 - MOBILE HOME

Notice that this unit is a single wide unit with a car port. There is an entrance road for easy access, and the property is located on a canal. If you were to advertise this property, you could get more rents than your typical unit as the water access is a great asset to this property, and you could get an extra $300 per month for this property.

The picture of the property is from 2003 which would be of a concern to me. I would want to have someone check out this property to be sure that the unit is still there and is in good condition. I personally do not have to go look at this property, but I would have someone do this for me and take several pictures. I look for a good mobile home park, something that offers amenities for the residents. I need to find out what the fees are if any and if there are any limitations or restrictions.

Single-family homes: These are the most desirable of all the properties as they offer the most exit strategies for an investor. If I were to get one of these, I could easily turn around and sell the unit to a family. I could resell it to an investor or keep it as a rental for cash flow. In some instances, I may sell the property to a homeowner by using the lease option technique or with owner financing.

Here is an example of a very nice single family home:

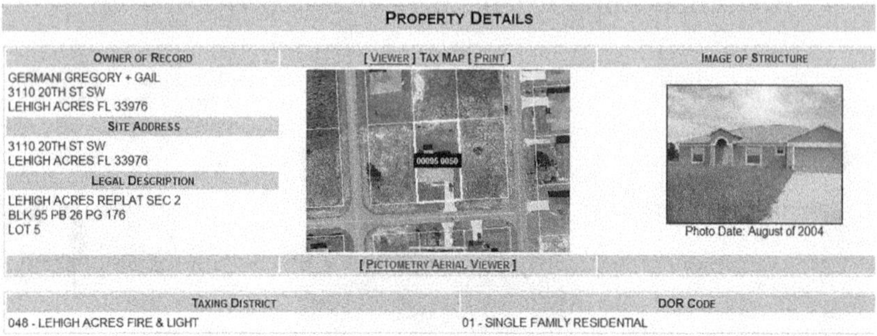
PROPERTY DETAILS

OWNER OF RECORD	[VIEWER] TAX MAP [PRINT]	IMAGE OF STRUCTURE
GERMANI GREGORY + GAIL 3110 20TH ST SW LEHIGH ACRES FL 33976 **SITE ADDRESS** 3110 20TH ST SW LEHIGH ACRES FL 33976 **LEGAL DESCRIPTION** LEHIGH ACRES REPLAT SEC 2 BLK 95 PB 26 PG 176 LOT 5	00095 0050	Photo Date: August of 2004
	[PICTOMETRY AERIAL VIEWER]	

TAXING DISTRICT	DOR CODE
048 - LEHIGH ACRES FIRE & LIGHT	01 - SINGLE FAMILY RESIDENTIAL

Notice how the home is in an area where few homes are located. That would mean that the area had some growth and currently has slowed or stopped. As an investor, that is desirable to me as this will help push up the demand for housing. When looking at these types of properties, I need to find out what the current market inventory level is holding at. I also want to find out what the competitive market rents are so I can decide if I am going to hold or sell this type of investment.

When looking at single-family homes, you need to check a few things before you purchase. You need to see if the heating and air-conditioning system is still installed. With many of the vacant properties, these items get stolen for their scrap value. I look for homes that have three bedrooms, two bathrooms, and a two-car garage. These are more likely to move quickly than if they did not have all of these attributes.

Multifamily homes: Investors love to pick up these types of properties as they have the potential for great cash flow. They are also easy to sell as you can get another investor pay top dollar if you can hold back of the financing.

Here is an example of a nice multifamily property:

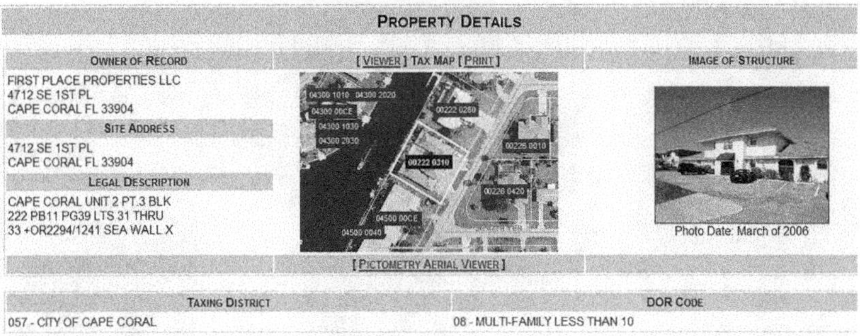

PROPERTY DETAILS

OWNER OF RECORD
FIRST PLACE PROPERTIES LLC
4712 SE 1ST PL
CAPE CORAL FL 33904

SITE ADDRESS
4712 SE 1ST PL
CAPE CORAL FL 33904

LEGAL DESCRIPTION
CAPE CORAL UNIT 2 PT.3 BLK
222 PB11 PG39 LTS 31 THRU
33 +OR2294/1241 SEA WALL X

[VIEWER] TAX MAP [PRINT]

[PICTOMETRY AERIAL VIEWER]

IMAGE OF STRUCTURE
Photo Date: March of 2006

TAXING DISTRICT	DOR CODE
057 - CITY OF CAPE CORAL	08 - MULTI-FAMILY LESS THAN 10

From the picture and the information provided by the county, I can see the property has six rental units. There is also a good access canal at the rear of the property which adds much value to this property. There is good parking at the front of the property and has a place for boats in the rear. With this asset, I can keep it, or I can resell it. I would probably look to keep it and see first the income it could generate. I need to determine the fixed cost and then subtract it from my income. I know that units like this will rent out for $800 per month and, with the six units, will bring in $4,800 per month. The fixed costs are estimated at $600 per month which would leave me with a positive cash flow of $4,200 per month. If I were to calculate that out, it would provide me with $57,600 in income per year. If I were to buy this unit for $75,000, I would see a 76.8% return the first year. I would go to the website "rentOmeter" to find the actual rents for the area and "Zillow" to get the value of the investment. After putting all of the information down on paper, I would then be able to decide on the best exit strategy once I purchased the property.

Commercial property: The use here is unlimited, and you only need to be aware of the inventory available and the location of the property. I have been looking at these for some time, and the first thing I check is to see where the property is located in the way of highway access. If I can find a building that is centrally located and is in fair to good condition, I will try to buy that property. If the location is poorly accessible and the building needs a lot of repairs, then I may not be so inclined to buy that property unless I got it at a real low price.

Here is an example of a good commercial property:

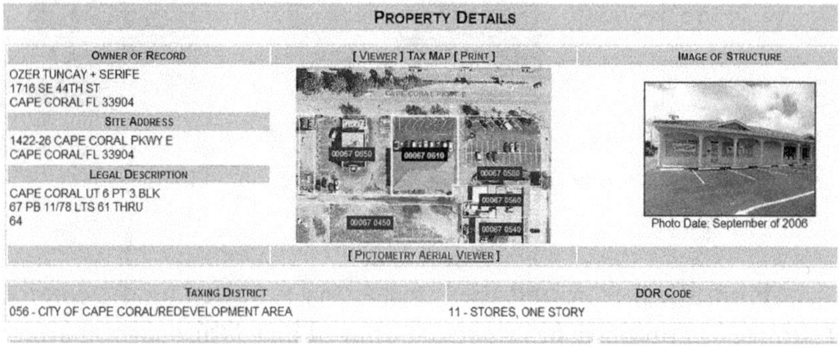

Notice that the building has a good frontal appearance and looks to be fairly new. Based on the map, I can tell that there is ample parking in the front, and there is another commercial building on either side. The area appears to be doing well, and after doing some research found, there is a need for commercial space. With this information in hand, this would make me interested in this property. I now need to find out what the rentals are for this area are and find that the rents are approximately $1,800 per month for a standard office unit with a frontage of twenty feet. The building is set up for three units, so that would have a potential monthly income of $5,400. Based on the cost of $700 per month, I estimate that this property would clear $47,700 per year. If I could buy this one for under $80,000, that would be a great deal. I would see a return of 70.5% ROI; this was calculated by dividing 56,400 (income)/$80,000 (price) = .705 x 100.

Agricultural: These have very low taxes and make for good places to plant your extra funds until the values increase. It is like farming. You buy the land based on the agricultural value and hold till the demand for land increases. Once the demand for buildable land increases, you then can see about getting the zoning use changed to residential. That will cause the land cost to increase dramatically.

Here is an example of an agricultural property:

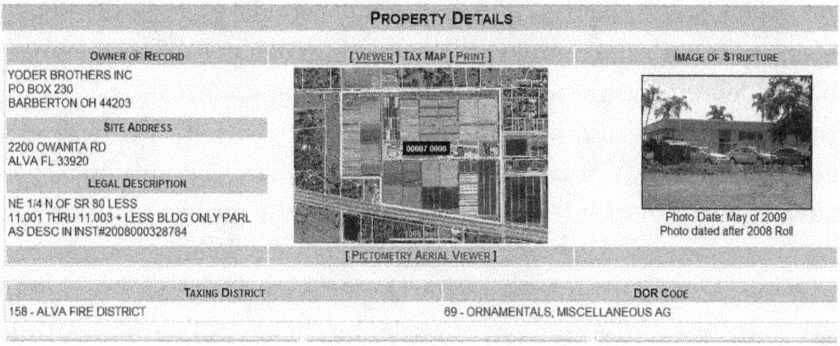

With this example on the previous page, there are roughly 107 acres of land associated with this property. The tax due on this type of property is $66,700 per year which is discounted based on the use.

The property is valued at over $10 million dollars, and the tax value is only $4.1 million dollars based on the deductions allowed for AG. If you were to hold this and wait to develop the land, you could potentially subdivide this into home sites at 1/4 acre parcels and sell them for $25,000 each.

After all your efforts, you could get about 180 home sites, and after setting up the infrastructure, you could possibly net $4,500.000.

That would mean that I would have to buy the property somewhere around $300,000 and hold for several years. If I had to leverage the money and wait, say, five years at pay 10% per year holding cost plus taxes, the total cost would be $150,000 in fees and another $333,500 in taxes.

My total outlay would be $483,500, and if I sold it for $4,500,000, I would see a profit of just over $4,000,000.

Not bad for a simple tax deed investment.

Step 3: Sale

The third step is learning how the sales are conducted. This is important in which you *must* understand the process or you can get yourself in much trouble.

Tax Lien Internet Auction

This process has built up desirability over the years and is offered in many states and counties across the United States. With the number of delinquent property owners not paying their real estate taxes, the numbers of sales have increased proportionately. The way this auction works is similar to that of "eBay" where the bids are set in advance. So let's start from the beginning of the process so we do not get you confused. The auctions typically will be conducted one time per year per taxing authority. Now I say taxing authority because in some regions of the country, the sales by the tax collector are at the local municipality level, while others are held at the county level. Now, the tax collector will promote the sale and must advertise this auction in a local general publication newspaper. This paper will be the one you see in the corner newspaper box or in the local community store or supermarket. The sale will be listed a minimum of three times which would be once per week. The day of the week will be the same day that they typically would run all the legal notices.

Now that we found the sale, we need to become a registered bidder for this auction. Just because you were a bidder in another county does not mean you are registered in this county to bid. Some taxing authorities require you to register each and every year, while others will let you keep the information active from year to year without the need to reregister. The process of registering is minimal and may only be a few pages long. The first thing that is required is the general information such as name, address, phone number, etc. Then you need to enter your tax ID number or EIN (employer identification number) and fill out the proper form from the IRS which is typically the W-9. When all that has been presented to the tax collector, they will process your application and give you your bidder number.

The auction process is different than most sales but is very similar to the way eBay auctions work. You go to the county bidder page that you have previously registered on and have deposited your minimum into the account, and you are ready to review the list of items.

With this website, you will find that most have links connected to the county tax collector, county appraiser, and possibly more. You can view the property, see the tax records, and, in some cases, see how many bids are currently on the parcel. I like the fact I can see how many bids are on the property because that will indicate if I will get the property or not. If I see that there are only three bids, I know I have a good chance to get the property. If there are three hundred bids, then I know my chances just became slim to none. I also know that as the sale proceeds to the end of the auction, many of the bidders will run out of money, and their bids will become void. This does not affect them in any way; it is just the county's way of limiting the bad bids or the bids that do not get paid. After winning the bids, I usually will have twenty-four hours to pay the remaining balance to the tax collector. If I were to forget to get the funds in, and I have done this before, they will sometimes give a call to see if I knew I had missed the payment deadline and give me a chance to pay the balance due. Either way, the tax collector will get paid.

Tax Lien Live Auction

The announcement of the live auction and the Internet auction is the same, and, therefore, I did not see the need to rewrite the same information twice. If you need to review that information again, please go back to the last section and see all the information there.

Next, you need to review the list and pick the liens you wish to bid on. Now here is where it gets interesting. The sale is held in a public location and is open to the general public. The auction will start in the morning after the start of business and before lunch. The time I have seem most commonly used is 10:00 a.m. for whatever the reason may be. Now here is where it gets real exciting. The sale will start with the tax collector making their typical announcements such as they have not owned the property, they have no knowledge of the property, and so forth. Then the sale will start with the first item on the list being called out for sale. The first item will be called out in several different methods. The typical way is when there are not many properties listed for sale. The first item will be called off this way:

The first property today is "Item number 1, lot 21, block 249, owners names are Pete Smith and Lisa Smith, and the property address is 1598 SW 87th Lane. The taxes due on this property are $1,459.98. Do I have any bids??

The group has the first bidder who calls out 18%.

This will be followed by, "I have a bid at 18%. Do I have any other bids?"

Hearing none, the tax collector will call out going once, going twice, sold for $1,459.98 to bidder number 2908.

If there were any other bids, the tax collector would entertain the bids as follows:

"I have 17%, any others bids? I have 16% over here, any others bids? I have 15% on this side, any others bids? I have 14% in the front, any other bids? OK, I have 14% going once. I have 14% going twice. Sold for 14%."

Now once the sale has concluded, the tax collector will announce when the funds need to be paid to the tax collector's office. This will usually be in the form of cash, cashier's check, certified funds, or a bank wire transfer. If any of the winning bidders fail to make it back by the time stipulated by the tax collector, they could forfeit their winning bids and possibly not be permitted back to the sale next year.

Tax Lien Over the Counter

Tax lien over the counter or advertised as they have been listed for sale before. These are the tax liens that were not sold the first time and will be available to any investor who makes the request and has the money. The lists can be requested from the tax collector, and they will make that list available. In some states, they do charge for these lists, and others just give it to you for free. I have seen a few counties offer the recent over-the-counter tax liens in a second auction within a few days to a few weeks of the first auction. This is a great way to pick up good liens before they have been picked through by every investor known to man.

Buying over the counter is just like buying at the sale, so you need to be registered in the same form as the other types of sales. The only difference is that you do not compete for the purchase of these tax liens.

The sale of the *over-the-counter* tax liens is a very simple process. You look over the list of the county-held tax lien certificates to see what is available. You pick out the ones you would like to buy and do whatever form of investigating you need to be comfortable in which to buy. You fill out your request on a piece of paper, a form issued by the tax collector or on one of your own forms you created. The request list will need the following information: your name, address, and phone number, the address of the property, tax lien number, and the legal designation for that property. That is all you need to do, and then send it to the tax collector's office for them to review. If the liens are available, they will contact you and give you the amount you need to get to the tax collector by a fixed date, and then the tax lien certificates are yours. No bidding, no completion, no worries.

Tax Deed Internet Auction

Tax deed auctions are listed on the Internet for the county and are also listed in the newspaper that the property will be sold for taxes. Most of the counties use an outside source to run these sales for the counties and offer the list of available properties a minimum of three weeks before the sale is to be conducted. With this, you can view the properties that are on the list as well as see which ones have been removed because they have either been paid off or the owners filed for bankruptcy protection.

To register for an online tax deed auction is the same as the online tax lien auctions. I have found that if a county offers the online tax lien certificate auction and they also offer the online tax deed auction, you do not have to reregister for that auction. Unfortunately, there are not too many states that offer both the tax deed and tax lien certificate sales, but Florida does, and they make it very easy for the investors to buy at their sales.

Process on how the sale is conducted is like every other Internet auction. The auction is set to take place on a certain date and a specific time. If there are many properties going up for sale, they will have several sale batches where there will be groups of properties sold at the specified time. It works like this: the first six hundred properties will be sold at 10:00 a.m., the second set of six hundred will be sold at 11:00 a.m., and so forth. Sometimes, they will go off in thirty-minute increments instead of the sixty-minute time increments. When the lists are smaller, they will start at a specific time, say 10:00 a.m., and each property is sold every two minutes to five minutes, and you may have the ability to watch the results online.

Tax Deed Live Auction

The live auctions always have an announcement in the newspaper indicating the number of parcels listed individually, the sequence of the sale number, and the taxes due. They may also list the owner's name and address of the property in the advertisement. The lists may also be available in the tax collector's office for you to review. At most of the live auctions, the tax collector will have an updated list available prior to the auction starting. This list can be used to see what has been removed and what is still available for sale.

The process to register is again like most other sales, and in some cases, you need to complete all paperwork prior to the sale starting, and other locations may not require you to do anything unless you win.

Tax deed live auctions are conducted in open public areas. This could mean anything from the tax collector's office to the steps of the county court's building. The sale process is to call off one property at a time until all the properties are sold. Some of the sales require payment of your winning bids at the conclusion of the sale, while others may require the payment immediately upon calling out the winning bid. In the state of Florida, they require you to immediately, upon winning the bid, go up to the tax collector and pay a $200 cash deposit for that property. They will print a receipt and log in your bid. If you were a winning purchaser in the past, your information will be on file, and they will move through this process fast. If this is the first time, the process takes longer. You are required to show an ID to the tax collector and a bidder registration form that is completed, and they enter your information as needed. They instruct you to bring back a certified check for each property you win and not to combine the checks into one for all the purchases.

Step 4: How

The final step is *how* you are going to bid on the properties at the auction. Each auction is unique in its own way, and a great investor knows how to bid for each of the different sales. Being an aggressive bidder at some sales does not always work for the entire sale types listed below.

Bidding at the Internet Tax Deed Auction

Tax deed sales online is new and exciting way to buy tax deed properties. For years, the only way to buy these types of properties was to go to an auction and stand among all the other investors and try to get a good deal if at all possible.

When I bid at these sales, I find it very easy to know how to get the best outcome possible. I can do the research and then place my highest and best bid amount. I try to put an amount that is less than 40% of the current market value. If I get the property, I know that I can resell it quickly and make a profit. The goal here is to make money many times over and not to try and make it all in one great big deal. I look for the properties that I feel will have less bidders and stay away from the ones that have many bidders. I look for the nice parcels of land that I can market and sell quickly to another investor. These are the parcels of land that I can get for under $5,000 and then relist them for $7,000 and make a small profit of $2,000. The strategy behind this is to do as many of these deals as you can and pocket the $2,000 per deal. Do this twice a month for a year, and you just made $48,000 with little effort and initial investment.

For the Florida online tax deed sales, I have been involved with the following:

https://www.lee.realtaxdeed.com, Lee County

https://www.charlotte.realforeclose.com/index.cfm, Charlotte County

https://www.duval.realforeclose.com/index.cfm, Duval County

https://www.manatee.realforeclose.com/index.cfm, Manatee County

https://www.walton.realforeclose.com/index.cfm, Walton County

Bidding at the Internet Tax Lien Auction

Internet tax lien auctions are similar to the tax deed auctions in that it is completely run by computer systems. The list is published on the Internet, and we get to put down our best offer on that property. In the case of the tax lien certificate sales, we are bidding on the lowest rate of interest we are willing to accept. The site permits the investor to place an interest rate they would like to receive, and all the other investors do the same.

The sites for the properties in Florida have a place where I can see how many people are bidding on a specific property. I can use this to my advantage as any property that has less than five bids on it will be a great potential. If we were all to place the same bid, the computer system will determine the winning bidder by using what is called random drawing.

I will place my limits for the sale, look over the list, and then make my best offer possible. I will set my limit and put forth many bids as possible and hope for the best. I find I get anywhere from 25% to 75% of all my bids accepted when I buy at this type of sale. I try to show where I can bid at 18% all day long and still expect to get many of the tax lien certificates I bid on. I have created a system where I sort the liens to find the ones very few investors want and still have the highest probability of redeeming within the two-year redemption period.

Many of the counties around the country with tax lien certificate sales offer some type of list, a way for all investors to buy at the auctions. I found that Arizona and Florida have the best sales available, and I like to frequent both of those states to buy tax liens.

I have been in most of the online Florida county tax lien certificate sales and attended many of the live tax deed sales. I have put together a list of the counties in Florida that offer the tax lien certificates for sale by way of an Internet auction.

Below, I have listed the counties I found in the state of Florida that offer tax lien certificate by way of an online sale.

Several also offer OTC sales.

Florida Internet Tax Auctions

County	*Website*
Alachua	http://www.alachuataxsale.com
Brevard	http://brevard.taxsale.com
Charlotte	http://charlotte.taxsale.com
Citrus	http://www.bidcitrus.com
Columbia	http://www.columbiataxsale.com
Duval	http://www.duvaltaxsale.com
Escambia	http://escambia.taxsale.com
Flagler	http://www.flaglertaxsale.com
Gadsden	http://www.gadsdentaxsale.com
Gilchrist	http://gilchrist.taxsale.com
Hernando	http://www.hernandotaxsale.com
Hillsborough	https://www.hillsboroughtaxsale.com
Indian River	http://www.indianrivertaxsale.com
Lake	http://www.bidlaketax.com
Lee	https://www.leetaxsale.com
Leon	http://www.bidleon.com

Levy	http://www.levytaxsale.com
Marion	http://www.bidmarion.com
Miami-Dade	http://www.bidmiamidade.com
Monroe	http://www.monroetaxsale.com
Nassau	http://www.nassautaxsale.com
Okaloosa	http://www.bidokaloosa.com
Orange	http://www.bidorangecounty.com
Osceola	http://www.bidosceola.com
Palm Beach	http://www.bidpbtc.com
Pinnellas	www.BidPinellas.com
Polk	http://polk.taxsale.com
Putnam	http://www.putnametaxsale.com
Santa Rosa	http://www.santarosataxsale.com
Sarasota	http://sarasota.taxsale.com
Seminole	http://www.seminoletaxsale.com
St. Johns	http://www.sri-auctiononline.com
St. Lucie	http://www.bidstlucie.com
Sumter	http://sumter.taxsale.com
Suwannee	http://www.suwanneetaxsale.com
Taylor	http://www.taylortaxsale.com
Volusia	http://www.bidvolusia.com
Walton	http://www.waltontaxsale.com

OTC (over-the-counter sales) if available are via the Internet.

Bidding at the Live Tax Deed Auction

The sales that I have attended over the years have been evolving every time I attend one. Back when I started, the sales were very competitive, and you had to work to get good deals. I had to use techniques like fast response bidding to keep my opponent off track as to where I would stop bidding. I also would bid in large increments to also put my adversary off guard.

Then, just when you had the system down, the attendance started to dwindle. At this point, all I had to do in order to get a good deal was to attend and open my mouth. The auctions then became a great place to get very good deals with little competition.

Then the cycle changed once more, and again, I had to compete with so many investors in order to get a good deal. The funny thing was all I had to do was go back to my old technique to get deals again. So I had to go back to fast bidding and pushing the increments out in large numbers. If my competitors were bidding in $100-dollar increments, I would go to $500-dollar increments.

Now, the fun begins, and we have gone again through another cycle. The investors have been staying home, and we again are able to pick the properties I want to buy. It is again a buyer's market. I have been going to the sales, and I see that there may only be ten investors, and of the ten, only five are actively bidding.

What has happened to the other investors? I can only imagine, and what I believe is that they are waiting for the next change to occur before they come back into the game. With that being said, it is the time to be in, or you will lose an opportunity that will not be around till the cycle changes again.

Bidding at the Live Tax Lien Auction

The live tax lien certificate sales are just like the deed sales in that investors act the same way at the same time. So when the tax deeds were attended by only a few investors, the same was so for the tax lien certificate sales. In this last cycle of the economy, the tax lien certificate sales had very low attendance.

I was recently in the Collier County, Florida, tax lien certificate sale and expected to have a lot of competition as this sale is a big draw for the investors. I was expecting to be there for three of the five days the auction was to take place, and since I wanted to get a good place at the sale, I arrived early. To my surprise, the sale was not overcrowded, just the opposite in that there were only about sixty people in the room that was set to hold over two hundred.

When the auction started, the numbers of bidders calling out were about twenty, and instead of getting one out of every fifty properties I bid on, I was getting one out of every ten. Not that I was complaining, but after only three hours at the auction, I had exhausted my entire three-day budget. This is a good thing, and I got the results I wanted in 1/6 of the time I had allotted. All of the tax liens I bid on were at 18%, and I was able to spend over $80,000 that morning.

If I had more of a budget, I could have bought even more of the tax lien certificates. At that sale I thought this is the time and the place to be purchasing the tax liens and the tax deeds.

My advice to you is to find out what sales they have in your area, learn the process, and start investing today. The investor that takes advantage today will benefit tomorrow, but those who wait to see what others are doing will always be watching from the sidelines.

CHAPTER 8

Develop Your Team

There are several things that you need to do when you start investing in tax liens and tax deeds as well as any other type of real estate investing, and that is to have a team in place to help you. Your team is made up of several people, and no one person is more important than the other, so I will just list them in a general order.

You need to have an accountant to handle your tax returns for you and your companies. The accountant is also a great source of private money lenders and may also be a private money lender.

Your realtor is also important because they can help you get the actual value for the properties you obtain from the tax lien or tax deed foreclosure. They can also help you when you are ready to sell because they may have other investors that are in the market for a property as well as a homeowner. The best part is that you can negotiate the commission they receive if you have been doing deals with them for some time now.

A mortgage broker is great to have because they know how to get us the money we need to do our deals. They are also important because when we want to sell our property after the foreclosure is completed, they can help our purchaser get the finances need to close the deal. Completing the foreclosure or setting up our company should be done by our attorney and that they are an integral part of our team. The more you use your attorney as well as referrals to others, the more discounts your attorney may give you.

Once we have a property and we decide to retail (fix up and sell for a higher profit) it, we need to have a good contractor on our team. As we get these properties and our contractor becomes more comfortable with us, we can either wholesale these properties to our contractor or just partner up with them.

A title company is also very important because we need to have the closing agent know how we buy, and as we do more deals with them, we will ask for a discount. Just imagine if we did several closings a year with the title company, would they not understand what we do and could they not lead us to potential deals as well?

Other investors are equally important as they may either buy from us or sell us properties. I like to have a database of qualified investors to offer my properties to and not have to wait for them to close. The more deals I do with them, the more I learn how and why they buy as well. The last on our list is OPM which stands for "other people's money." I hear a lot of investors talk about it, but very few go into detail on how to find it. What you need to do is surround yourself with individuals who think and act like yourself with respect to investing. It may not necessarily be real estate investing, but the mind frame of these individuals will be the same as yours. They will lead you to OPM and may be the ones to lend you the money. You need to have a business plan and be able to explain how you intend on using their money and the returns they can expect to receive.

How to Invest Inside Your Self-Directed Roth IRA

Why not open up a self-directed Roth IRA (SDRIRA) where your annual contribution are limited to $7,000 if your single if your married as of 2019 where it was increased from $3,000 in 2004. There is one company located in Ohio that is the leader in using the Roth IRAs by the name of equity trust. There Internet site is www.trustetc.com, and you can find out much information on this product and how they can help you build unlimited amounts of wealth.

All of your contributions placed into your self-directed Roth IRA are taxed before they are deposited, and, therefore, all of your profits are going to be tax-free. One of the requirements with the SDRIRA is that you cannot withdraw any funds from the account without 10% penalty until you are at least 59.5 years of age (exceptions: death, disability, first-time home purchases), and your account has been open for at least five years. In the SDRIRA, you do not have to make required minimum distributions by age 70.5 that you would if you have a traditional IRA. Contributions are limited in all of the IRAs available to us, but the greatest part is that the profit is unlimited! These are also good vehicles for protecting your future from lawsuits and judgments in most states as they cannot go after an individual's IRA.

Any consideration must come from the SDRIRA and not your personal account. All profits including cash flow from rentals must go into SDRIRA. Equity trust can overnight paper work and funds to lock up deals. You can lend to others, but you cannot do deals with parents, grandparents, or parents of linear decent. You can, however, do deals with brothers, sisters, friends, business people, or anyone else who may be interested.

What you need to do is to open your self-directed Roth IRA and purchase the investment with the money in the SD Roth IRA in the name of the IRA. That is something that equity trust can help you with such as getting you all the paperwork needed and sending the checks on your behalf to the third party. When the property is sold, the profit is then deposited back into your SDRIRA without being taxed again.

Now, you go out and purchase the tax lien in the name of your SDRIRA. When the tax lien is redeemed or you sell the property, that profit goes back into the SDRIRA without ever being taxed. If you assign the tax lien to another investor, then the profits from that transaction go into the SD Roth IRA without being taxed such as if you lock up the purchase of the tax lien with a $100 and then assign it to another investor for $5,000, then the $5,000 goes back into your SDRIRA, all tax-free. Some of the advantages are that all of the qualified withdrawals are tax-free, there are no required withdrawals, and you are able to pass earnings to beneficiary's tax free. You can also buy and sell, buy and hold, lend to partners or build private banks, and lend out to another investors.

Power of Compounding Interest

Let's look at an example where you use your SDRIRA to buy tax liens in the state of Texas where the interest rate is a 25% penalty every six months for nonowner-occupied properties and 25% per year on the rest. As part of our strategy, we target nonowner-occupied properties so we can get the 25% every six months. We first go to the sale, and we buy a tax deed for $8,000, and within the next six months, it redeems and pays $10,000 back to your SDRIRA. Since Texas has tax sales on the first Tuesday of every month, we can take our funds and repeat the process.

Now, you invest that full amount and buy a tax deed for $10,000, and, again, within the next six months, it redeems and pays $12,500 back to your SDRIRA. Then you buy another tax deed for $12,500, and, again, within the next six months, it redeems and pays $15,625 back to your SDRIRA. In six years, your SDRIRA will be worth $93,132.26, and in just ten years, it will be worth $555,111.00. Would that help you when you retire if you could take an amount of $8,000 and have it grow to $555,111 in just ten years? *Wow*, can you imagine what it would be worth if you only got one of the properties instead of it redeeming? The potential is mind-blowing when you think of how much money one can have tax free when they retire.

How to Run Your Own Business

Organize

Like any business you start, there are certain habits you need to have or develop. Being organized is very important, and if you're not organized, you will become distracted or go off of your course or plan. Take out your calendar, personal planner, or computer organizer and put down what you need to do every day. If you write these things down, you are more likely to accomplish these tasks. Although they say a messy desk is a sign of genius, just look at who is telling you that, the person with the messy desk. Keep your appointments on time, send out all of your correspondences on time, and file important papers in the correct place.

Follow-Up

The greatest mistake people make when they first start out is not calling people back when they left a message or not follow-up on an offer you made that was not accepted. If you contact someone who has several tax liens for sale and they are not interested in selling any to you today, make sure you mark your calendar to call him back in the next thirty to sixty days to see if they had a change in their circumstances. If you follow up on the offers you make, you will have a higher probability of getting deals.

Accounting

Most people don't know how to do their own taxes, and I am no different. You need to have an accountant that understands real estate investing to make sure you get all the benefits you are entitled to. Next, you need to keep track of your own accounting such as a checkbook. One mistake many investors make is to commingle funds, and then they lose their corporate protection. One system of accounting you may want to use is QuickBooks as that is what my accountant told me to use because that is what she uses. At the end of the year, all I do is back up my QuickBooks file and email it to her; it is that simple.

Plan for Your Retirement

One thing I found while I have been out training investors around the country is that they have not planned for retirement.

What most people do is fail to plan for the future by waiting to start. Why not pay yourself first from every deal or paycheck you get instead of wasting it on things that you don't really need like the extra pack of cigarettes or that coffee or latte? By doing this, you will find yourself saving money and getting ready for retirement. But what I see is that most everyone pays the household bills first and then the miscellaneous expenses and then they find themselves out of money before the next pay day. Why not pay yourself first by say $1 for every hour of work you put in? In one week, that would be $40, in one year, that would be $2,080, and in ten years, that would be $20.800. But if you were to invest that same amount of money at only 10%, you would have about $36,464.

It is unfortunate that most people who retire today end up at or below the poverty level because they do not have enough for retirement. It is not because they did not plan nor is it because they did not work hard all of their lives. It is because the cost of living has risen more than what they have put aside for those wonderful golden years. What most end up doing is getting a part-time job to supplement their income, and we have all seen them at department stores or fast food joints which is not where they need to be. I have planned for the future and have followed my plan to where I know my wife and I will be able to retire comfortably and not have to do anything but play golf, go motorcycle riding, or take the afternoon for boating.

I am on what I call the 40-40-40 plan. I have worked since I was ten years old, so I will stop at the age of fifty and stay retired for the next forty years. At that time, if I so desire, I will try to work for the next forty years (but don't count on it as am sure I will enjoy being retired).

CHAPTER 9

State by State Directory

Legal disclaimer: The following information was taken from several sources and should not be taken as legal advice or in place of advice from your local real estate or tax lien attorney. You should still check with your tax collector in the county in which you will be investing your money into tax liens and tax deeds.

Tax Lien States

Alabama
Arizona
Colorado
DC
Illinois
Indiana
Iowa
Kentucky
Louisiana
Maryland
Mississippi
Missouri
Montana
Nebraska
New Jersey
Oklahoma
South Carolina
South Dakota
West Virginia
Wyoming

Tax Deed States

Alaska
Arkansas
California
Connecticut (r)
Delaware (r)
Georgia (r)
Hawaii (r)
Idaho
Kansas
Maine
Michigan
Minnesota
New Hampshire
New Mexico
North Carolina
North Dakota
Oregon
Pennsylvania
Rhode Island (r)
Tennessee (r)
Texas (r)
Utah
Wisconsin
Vermont (r)
Virginia
Washington

(r) indicates that is a redeemable deed state

Tax lien and deed states (aka hybrid states)

Florida

- Liens held once a year.
- Deeds are held monthly; no redemption.

Massachusetts

- Liens may be sold by bulk sales once a year.
- Deeds are held year round, with redemption.

Nevada

- Liens held once a year on special assessments.
- Deeds are held monthly; no redemption.

New York

- Liens held once a year, mostly at private auctions.
- Deeds are held year round; no redemption.

Ohio

- Liens held once a year, mostly at private auctions.
- Deeds are held year round; no redemption.

Specific State Information

Alabama

- Sold by the county; forty-two counties.
- Tax lien sales only.
- Sales held annually, usually around May.
- 12% annual rate of return.
- Three years from date of sale is the redemption period.
- Highest bid over lien amount wins the tax lien.
- You get back your premium if the lien redeems.
- They sell over-the-counter liens, "OTC."
- OTC typically offered by the property tax division.

State flag

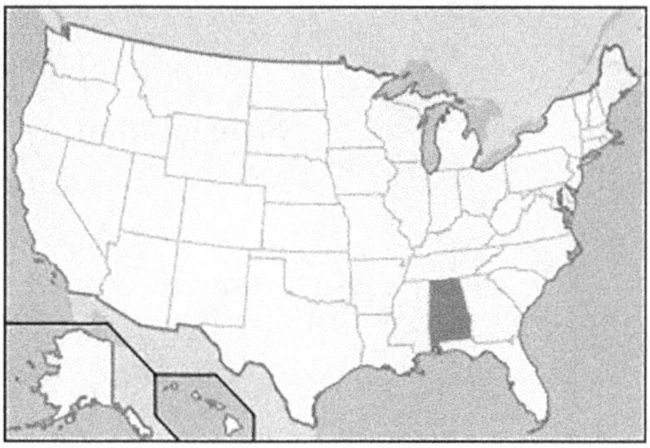

Map location

Alaska

- Sold by the county and cities.
- Twelve counties and thirteen cities hold sales.
- Tax deed sales only.
- Sales held year round; varies as to the dates.
- No redemption period if tax deed purchased.
- No annual rate of return, you get the deed.
- Highest bid over tax lien amount wins the deed.
- Assessors typically hold the auctions.

State flag

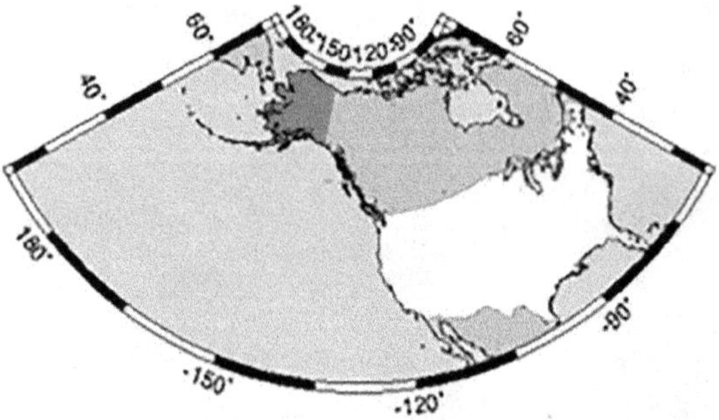

State location

Arizona

- Sold by the county, fifteen counties.
- Tax lien sales only.
- Sales held annually, usually on February 1.
- 16% annual rate of return.
- Three years from date of sale is the redemption period.
- Lowest interest bid wins the tax lien.
- All subsequent tax liens paid earn initial interest.
- They sell over-the-counter liens, "OTC."
- OTC typically offered by the tax collector.

State flag

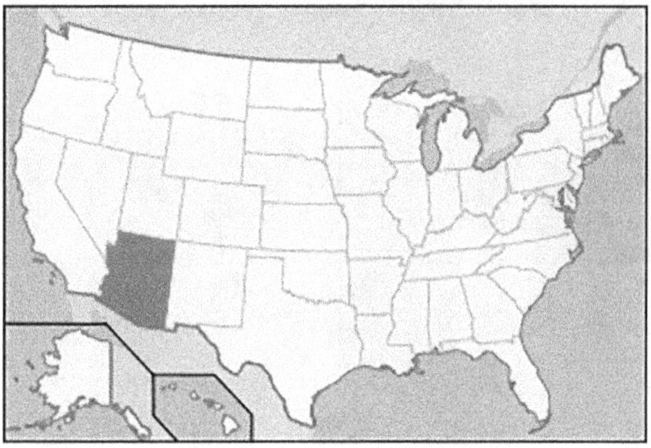

State location

Arkansas

- Sold by the county, seventy-five counties.
- Tax deed sales only.
- Sales held quarterly.
- No redemption period after thirty days from the date the tax deed was purchased.
- No annual rate of return, you get the deed.
- Highest bid over tax lien amount wins the deed.
- Commissioner typically holds the auctions.

State flag

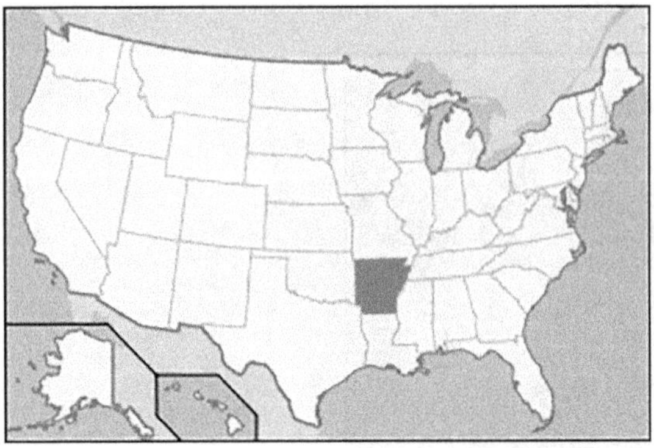

State map

California

- Sold by the county, fifty-eight counties.
- Tax deed sales only.
- Sales held once to twice a year, February and August.
- No redemption period after the tax deed sale.
- No annual rate of return, you get the deed.
- Highest bid over tax lien amount wins the deed.
- Property owner can be five years behind in taxes before a property will be offered for sale.

State flag

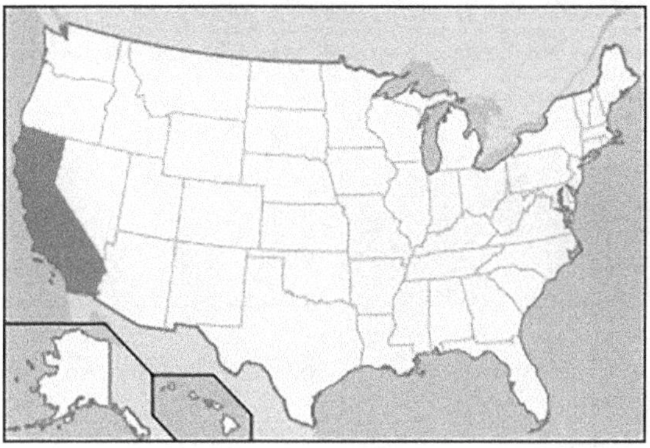

State map

Colorado

- Sold by the county, sixty-four counties.
- Tax lien sales only.
- Sales held annually, usually around November.
- 9% over the fed discount rate as set in September is the rate of return.
- Three years from date of sale is the redemption period.
- Highest bid over lien amount wins the tax lien.
- You do *not* get back your premium if the lien redeems.
- They sell over-the-counter liens, "OTC."
- OTC typically offered by the property tax division.

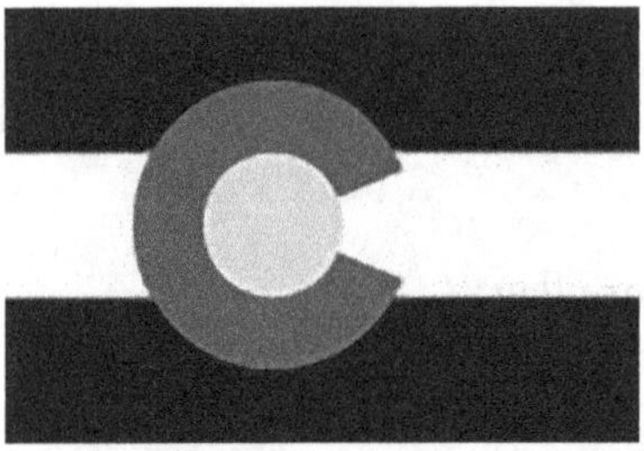

State flag

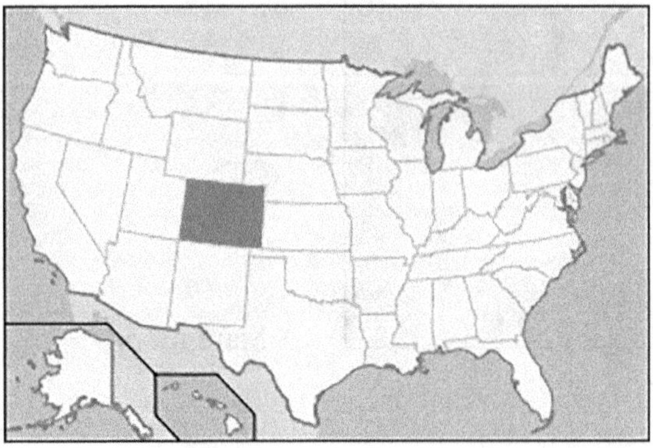

State map

Connecticut

- Sold by the municipality, 169 municipalities.
- Tax deed sales only.
- Sales held annually, usually around June.
- No redemption period after one year from the date the tax deed was purchased.
- 18% rate of return if tax deed is redeemed.
- Highest bid over tax lien amount wins the deed.
- Deed held and not recorded for one year.

State flag

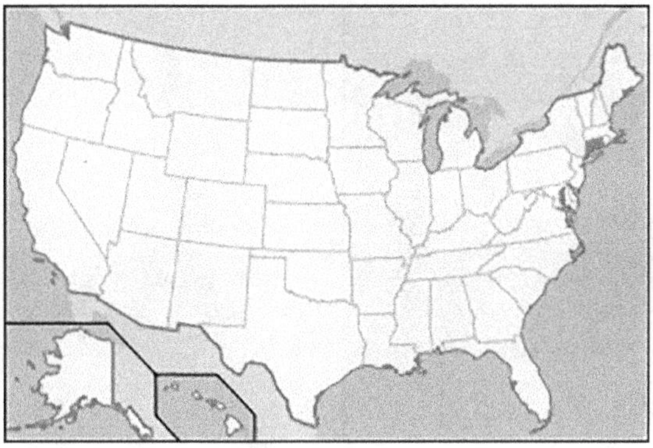

State map

Delaware

- Sold by the county, three counties.
- Tax deed sales only.
- Sales can be held monthly.
- No redemption period after one year from the date the tax deed was purchased.
- 15%–20% annual rate of return, you get the deed.
- Highest bid over tax lien amount wins the deed.

State flag

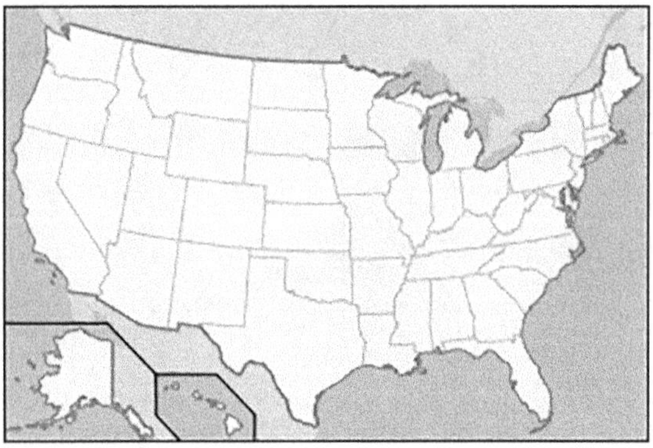

State map

District of Columbia

- Sold by the county, only one district here.
- Tax lien sales only.
- Sales held annually, usually around May.
- 1.5% per month rate of return.
- Six months from date of sale is the redemption period.
- Highest bid over lien amount wins the tax lien.
- You get back your premium if the lien redeems.
- They do not sell over-the-counter liens, "OTC."
- OTC typically offered by the property tax division.

State flag

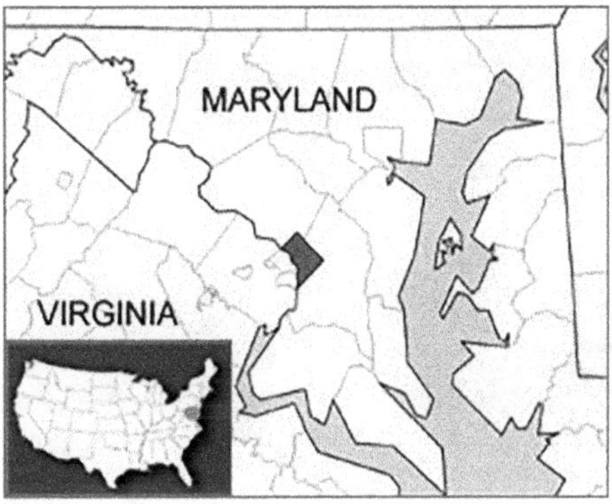

State map

Florida

- Sold by the county, sixty-seven counties.
- Tax lien sales held annually, usually around May.
- 18% annual rate of return.
- Minimum interest of 5% earned if bid is over 0.
- Two years from date of sale is the redemption period.
- Lowest interest rate bid wins the tax lien.
- They sell over-the-counter liens, "OTC."
- OTC typically offered by the tax collector.

State flag

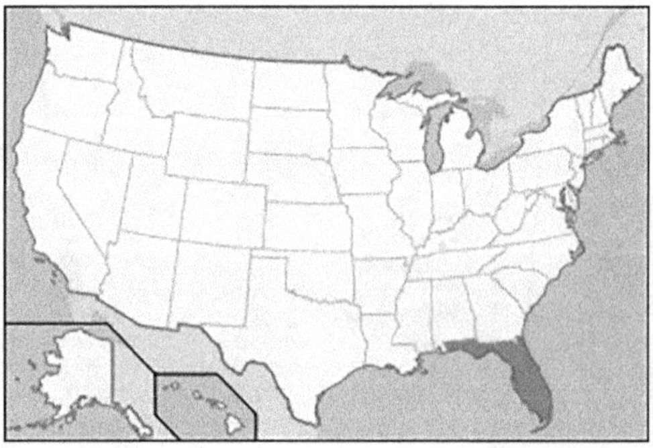

State map

Florida
Tax deed sales are held monthly.

- No redemption period after the date the tax deed sale.
- No annual rate of return, you get the deed.
- Highest bid over tax lien amount wins the deed.
- County clerk typically holds the auctions.
- Online auctions for deeds and liens.

Georgia

- Sold by the county, 159 counties.
- Tax deed sales only.
- Sales held monthly, first Tuesday of the month.
- No redemption period after the date the tax deed was purchased.
- 20% rate of return, you get the deed.
- Highest bid over tax lien amount wins the deed.
- Must stop the redemption period; possession immediate.

State flag

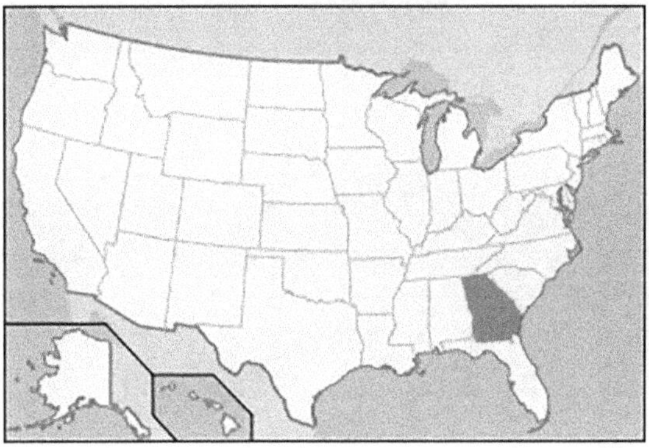

State map

Hawaii

- Sold by the county, four counties.
- Tax deed sales only.
- Sales held annually.
- No redemption period after one year from the date the tax deed was recorded.
- 12% annual rate of return, first year only.
- Highest bid over tax lien amount wins the deed.
- The Department of Finance typically holds the auctions.

State flag

State map

Idaho

- Sold by the county, forty-four counties.
- Tax deed sales only.
- Sales held annually.
- No redemption period after the date the tax deed was purchased.
- No annual rate of return, you get the deed.
- Highest bid over tax lien amount wins the deed.

State flag

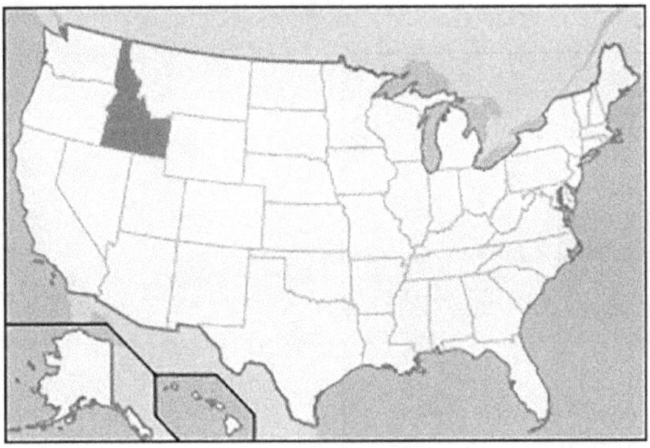

State map

Illinois

- Sold by the county, 102 counties.
- Tax lien sales only.
- Sales held annually, usually around the summer.
- 18% semiannual rate of return.
- Two years from date of sale is the redemption period.
- Lowest interest rate bid wins the tax lien.
- You get back your premium if the lien redeems.
- They sell over-the-counter liens, "OTC."
- Some counties sell tax-deeded properties.

State flag

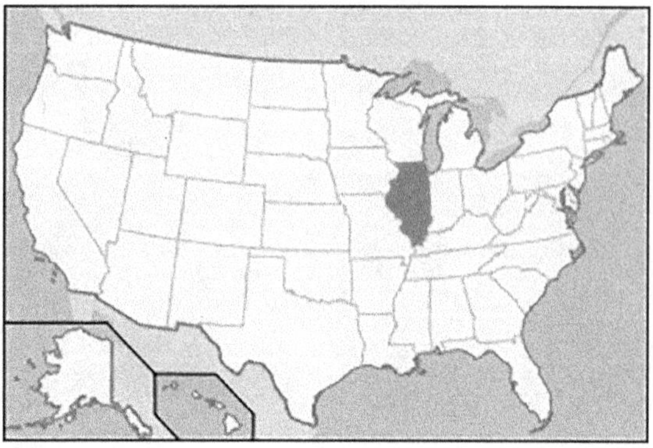

State map

Indiana

- Sold by the county, ninety-two counties.
- Tax lien sales only.
- Sales held annually, usually around September.
- 10% < six months.
- 15% >six months < twelve months.
- 25% > twelve months.
- One year from date of sale is the redemption period.
- Highest bid over lien amount wins the tax lien.
- You get back your premium if the lien redeems.
- They sell over-the-counter liens, "OTC."

State flag

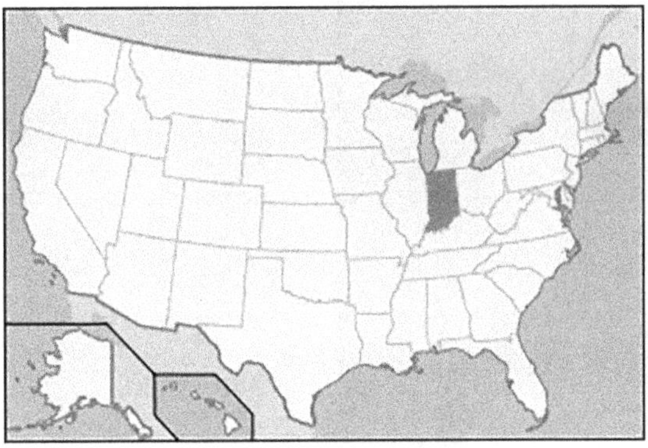

State map

Iowa

- Sold by the county, ninety-nine counties.
- Tax lien sales only.
- Sales held annually, usually around July.
- 2% per month rate of return.
- Twenty-one months from date of sale is the redemption period.
- Round robin and percent ownership bid on liens.
- They sell over-the-counter liens, "OTC."
- OTC typically offered by the tax division.

State flag

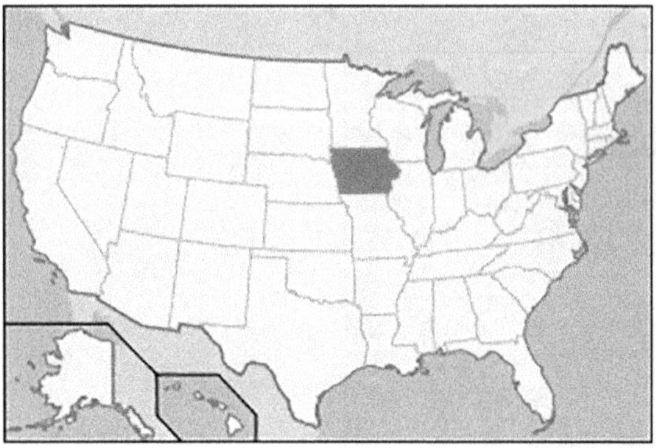
State map

Kansas

- Sold by the county, 105 counties.
- Tax deed sales only.
- Sales held typically year round.
- No redemption period after the date the tax deed was purchased.
- No annual rate of return, you get the deed.
- Highest bid over tax lien amount wins the deed.
- County treasurer typically holds the auctions.

State flag

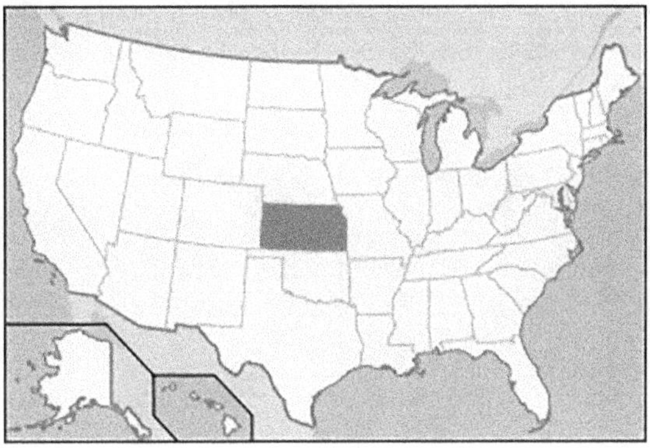

State map

Kentucky

- Sold by the county, 120 counties.
- Tax lien sales only.
- Sales held annually.
- 12% annual rate of return.
- One year from date of sale is the redemption period.
- First to bid and lowest interest rate bid wins the tax lien.
- Some counties sell over-the-counter liens, "OTC."

State flag

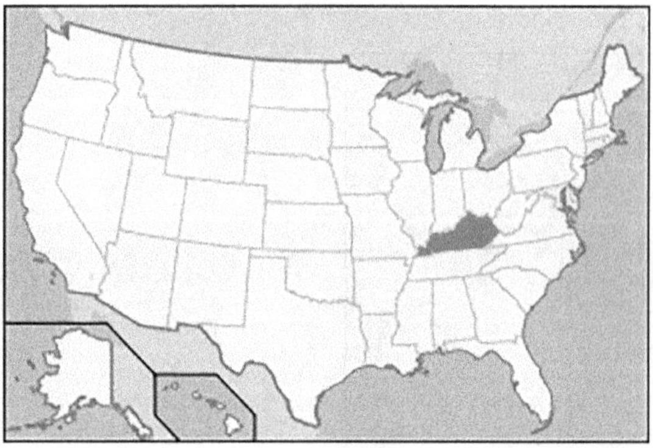

State map

Louisiana

- Sold by the parish, sixty-four parishes.
- Tax lien sales only.
- Sales held annually, usually around May.
- 5% penalty + 1% monthly rate of return.
- Three years from date of sale is the redemption period.
- Lowest interest rate bid and percent ownership wins the tax lien.
- Few parishes sell over-the-counter liens, "OTC."
- OTC typically offered by the property tax division.

State flag

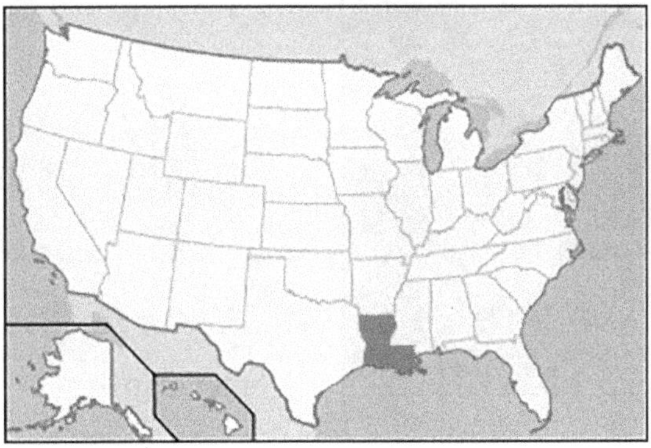

State map

Maine

- Sold by the municipality, 492 counties.
- Tax deed sales only.
- Sales held year round.
- No redemption period after the date the tax deed was purchased.
- No annual rate of return, you get the deed.
- Highest bid over tax lien amount wins the deed.
- The tax collector typically holds the auctions.

State flag

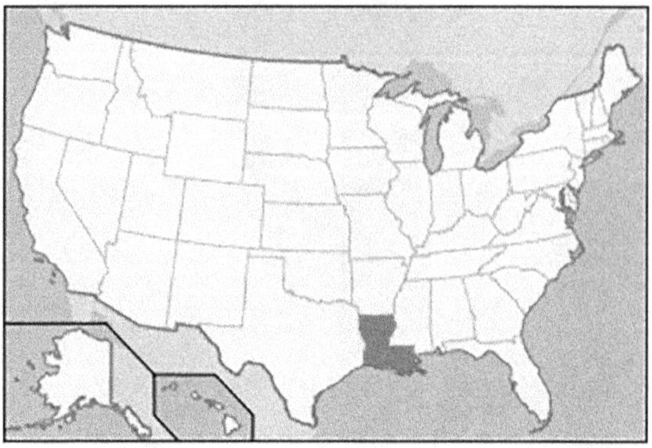

State map

Maryland

- Sold by the county, twenty-three counties.
- Tax lien sales only.
- Sales held annually, usually around May.
- 12%–24% annual rate of return by county.
- Six to twenty-four months from date of sale is the redemption period depending on the county.
- Highest bid over lien amount wins the tax lien.
- You get back your premium if the lien redeems.
- Liens not foreclosed in two years are void.

State flag

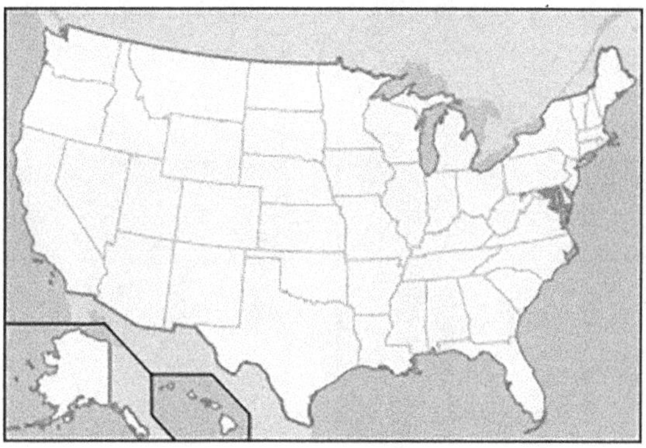

State map

Massachusetts

- Tax lien sales (aka tax taking).
- Counties usually take these liens to foreclosure.
- Sold by the county, fourteen counties.
- Tax deed sales.
- Sales held different times during the year.
- No redemption period after the date the tax deed was purchased.
- No annual rate of return, you get the deed.
- Highest bid over tax lien amount wins the deed.

State flag

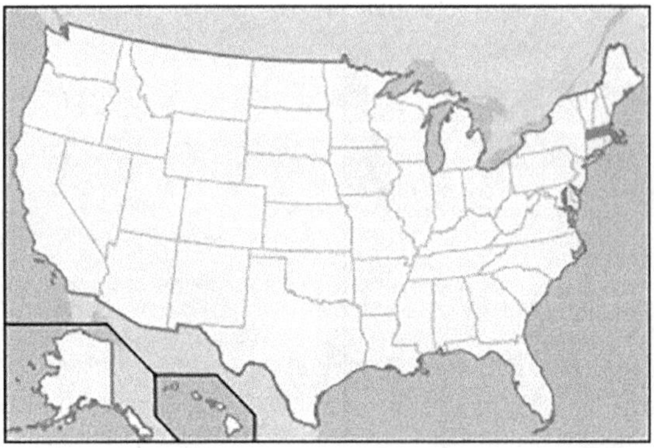

State map

Michigan

- Sold by the county, eighty-three counties.
- Tax deed sales only after 2006.
- Sales held year round.
- No redemption period after the date the tax deed was purchased.
- No annual rate of return, you get the deed.
- Highest bid over tax lien amount wins the deed.

State flag

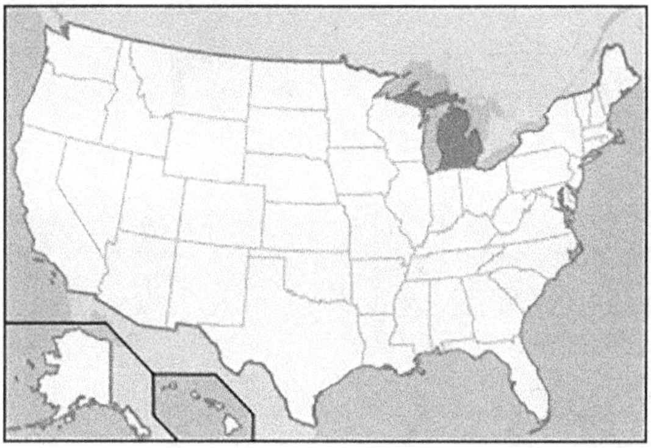

State map

Minnesota

- Sold by the county, eighty-seven counties.
- Tax deed sales only.
- Sales held year round.
- No redemption period after the date the tax deed was purchased.
- No annual rate of return, you get the deed.
- Highest bid over tax lien amount wins the deed.
- The sell over-the-counter liens, "OTC."

State flag

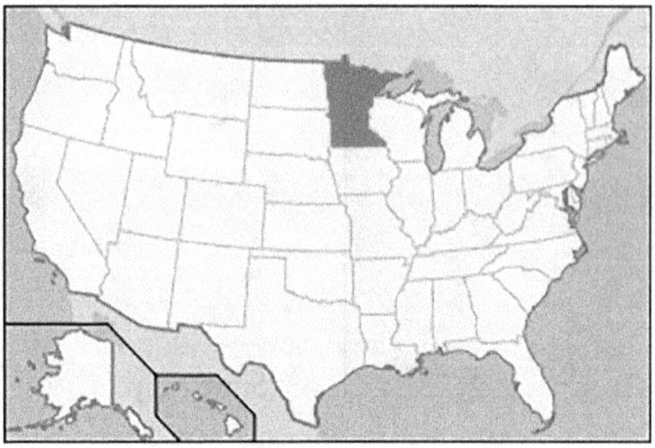

State map

Mississippi

- Sold by the county, eighty-two counties.
- Tax lien sales only.
- Sales held biannual, usually around April and August.
- 17%–18% annual rate of return by county on taxes.
- Two years from date of sale is the redemption period.
- Highest bid over lien amount wins the tax lien.
- You do *not* get back your premium if the lien redeems.
- They sell over-the-counter liens, "OTC."

State flag

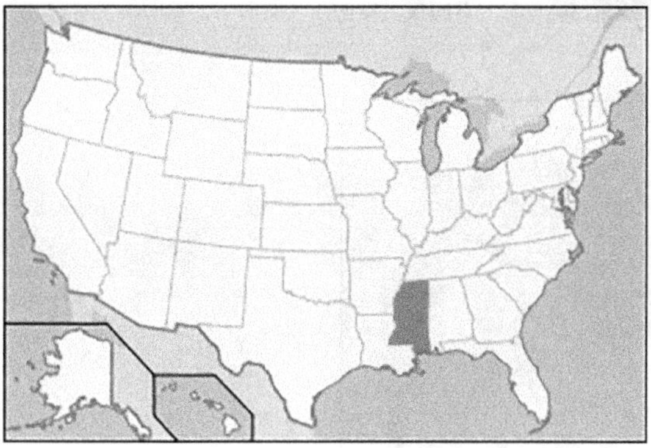

State map

Missouri

- Sold by the county, 136 counties.
- Tax lien sales only.
- Sales start the fourth Monday of August.
- 10% annual rate of return.
- One year from date of sale is the redemption period.
- Third sale has only ninety-day redemption period.
- Highest bid over lien amount wins the tax lien.
- You get back your premium if the lien redeems.
- They sell over-the-counter liens, "OTC."
- OTC typically offered by the property tax division.

State flag

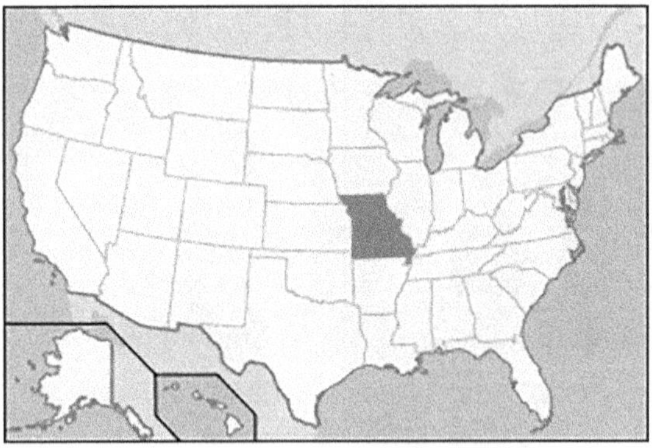

State map

Montana

- Sold by the county, fifty-six counties.
- Tax lien sales only.
- Sales held annually, usually around June or July.
- 10% annual rate of return.
- Three years (buildings) and two years (land) from the date of sale are the redemption periods.
- First to offer minimum bid wins.
- They sell over-the-counter liens.

State flag

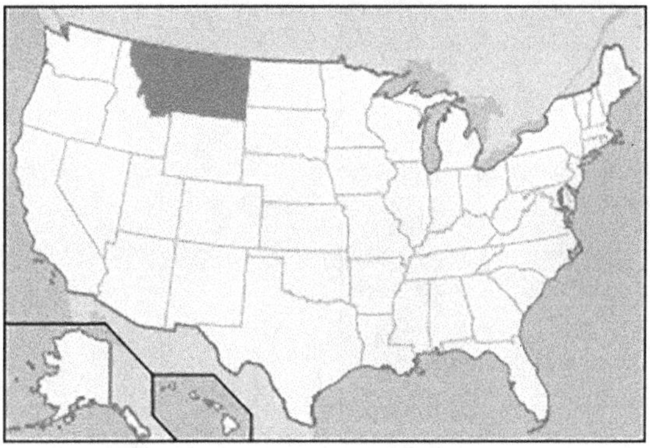

State map

Nebraska

- Sold by the county, ninety-three counties.
- Tax lien sales only.
- Sales held annually, usually around March.
- 14% annual rate of return.
- Three years from date of sale is the redemption period.
- Rotational bid wins the tax lien.
- They sell over-the-counter liens, "OTC."
- OTC typically offered by the tax department.

State flag

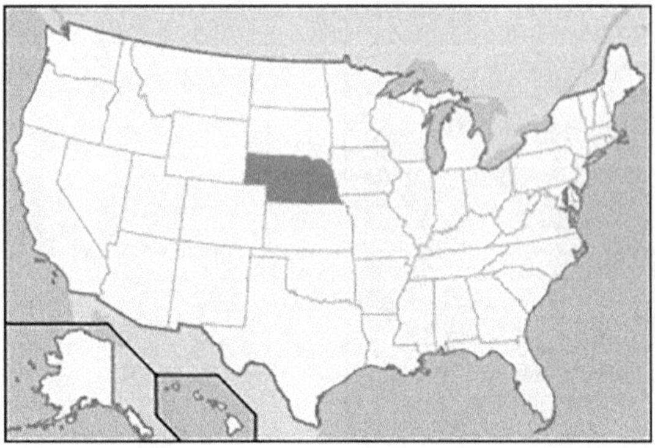

State map

Nevada

- Sold by the county, seventeen counties.
- Tax lien sales (on special assessments only).
- Sales held annually, usually around April.
- 12% annual rate of return.
- 120 days for land and two years on improved property are the redemption periods.
- Highest bid over lien amount or lottery bid wins.
- They sell over-the-counter liens.

State flag

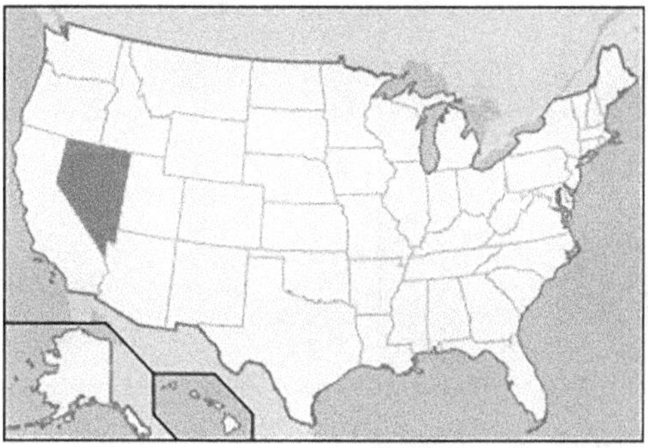

State map

Nevada

- Tax deed sales.
- Sales can be held quarterly.
- No redemption period after the date the tax deed was purchased.
- No annual rate of return, you get the deed.
- Highest bid over tax lien amount wins the deed.

New Hampshire

- Sold by the municipality, 234 municipalities.
- Tax deed sales only.
- Sales held year round; varies as to the dates.
- No redemption period if tax deed purchased.
- No annual rate of return, you get the deed.
- Highest bid over tax lien amount wins the deed.
- Assessors typically hold the auctions.

State flag

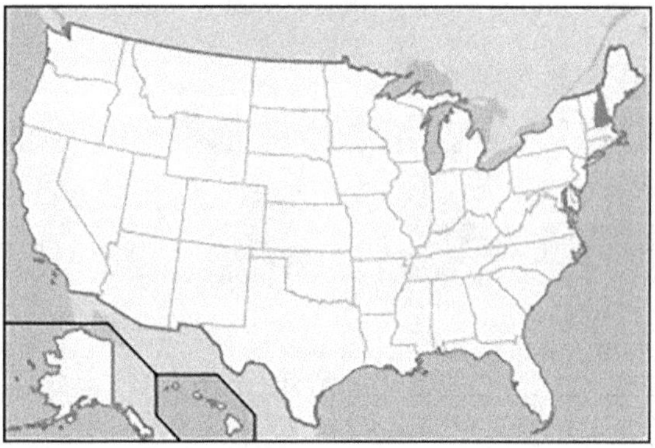

State map

New Jersey

- Sold by the municipality, 567 municipalities.
- Tax lien sales only.
- Sales held annually, months vary
- 18% annual rate of return.
- Two years from date of sale is the redemption period.
- Lowest interest bid over lien amount wins the tax lien.
- You get back your premium if the lien redeems within five years of buying the lien.
- They sell over-the-counter liens, "OTC."

State flag

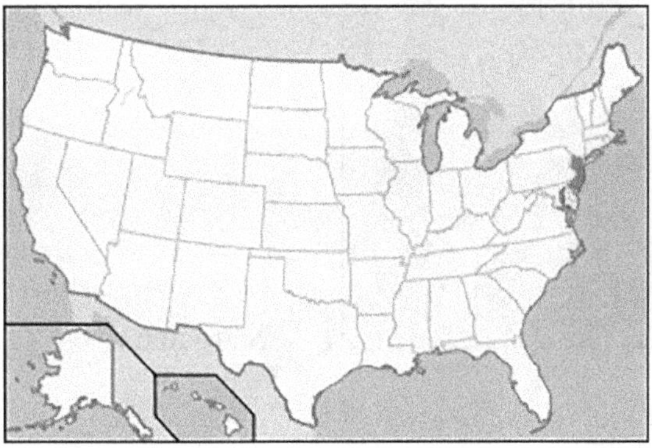

State map

New Mexico

- Sold by the county, thirty-two counties.
- Tax deed sales only.
- Sales held year round; varies as to the dates.
- No redemption period if tax deed purchased.
- No annual rate of return, you get the deed.
- Highest bid over tax lien amount wins the deed.
- In some counties, the mortgage survives the sale.

State flag

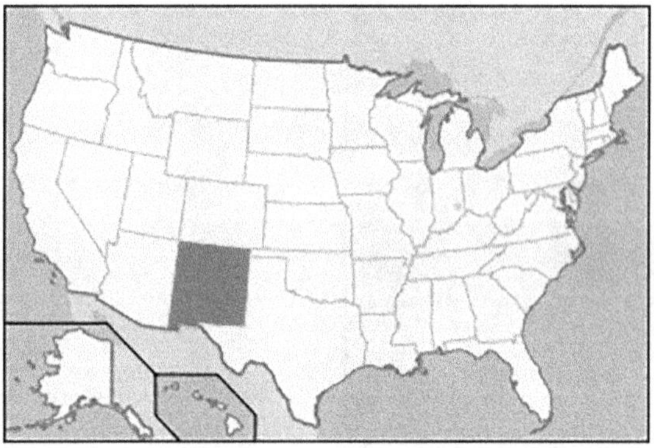

State map

New York

- Sold by the county, sixty-two counties.
- Tax lien sales.
- Sales held annually; usually a private auction.
- 14% annual rate of return.
- Approximately one year is the redemption period.
- Highest bid over lien amount wins the tax lien.
- You get back your premium if the lien redeems.
- They sell over-the-counter liens, "OTC."
- Most counties sell tax deeds instead of liens.

State flag

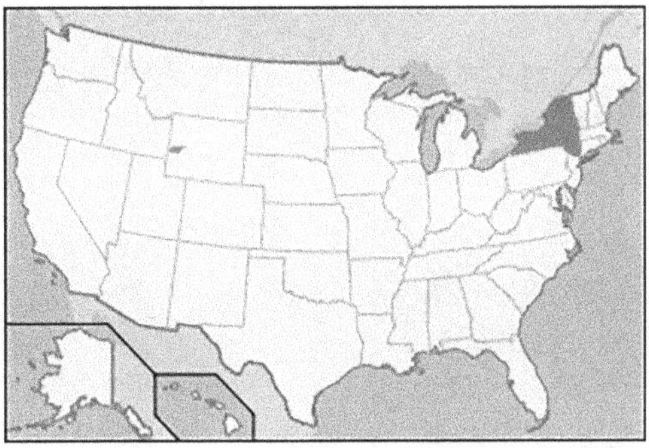

State map

New York

- Tax deed sales.
- Sales held year round; varies as to the dates.
- No redemption period if tax deed purchased.
- No annual rate of return, you get the deed.
- Highest bid over tax lien amount wins the deed.
- The tax collector typically holds the auctions.

North Carolina

- Sold by the county, 109 counties.
- Tax deed sales only.
- Sales held year round, usually monthly.
- No redemption period if tax deed purchased.
- Confirmation of sale subject to upset bid by others within ten days from the sale. Must be 5% higher.
- No annual rate of return, you get the deed.
- Highest bid over tax lien amount wins the deed.

State flag

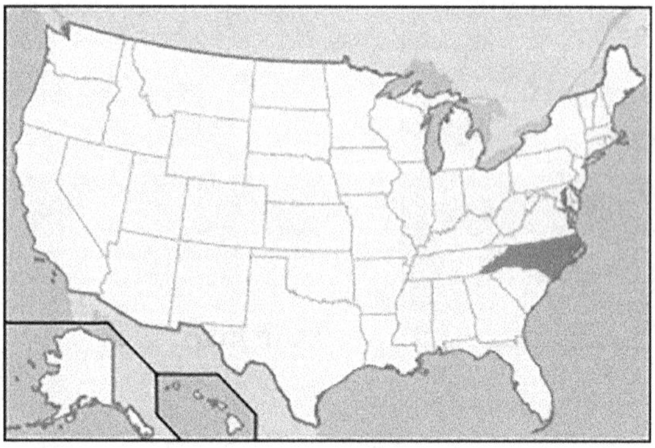

State map

North Dakota

- Sold by the county, fifty-three counties.
- Tax deed sales.
- Sales held annually; varies but usually in November.
- No redemption period if tax deed purchased.
- No annual rate of return, you get the deed.
- Highest bid over tax lien amount wins the deed.
- The tax collector typically holds the auctions.

State flag

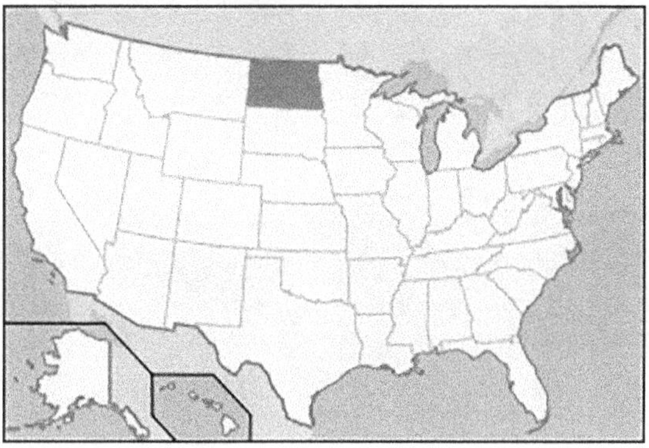
State map

Ohio

- Sold by the county, eighty-eight counties.
- Tax lien sales for institutional buyers (bulk).
- 18% interest earned annually if tax lien redeems.
- One year from the date of sale is the redemption period.
- Lowest interest rate bid wins the lien.
- The tax collector typically holds the auctions.

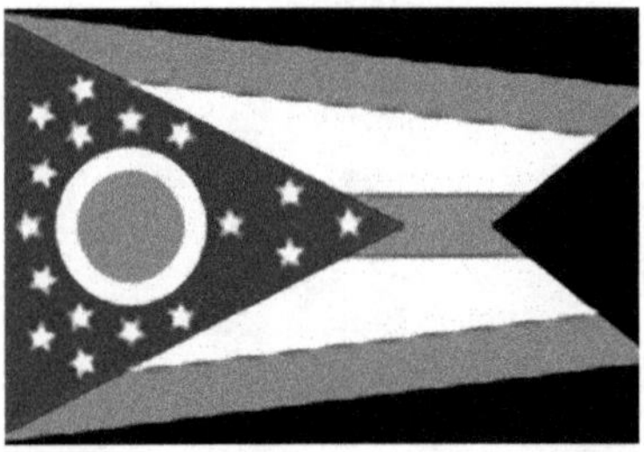

State flag

State map

Ohio

- Tax deed sales.
- Sales held year round; varies as to the dates.
- No redemption period if tax deed purchased.
- No annual rate of return, you get the deed.
- Highest bid over tax lien amount wins the deed.
- The tax collector typically holds the auctions.

Oklahoma

- Sold by the county, seventy-seven counties.
- Tax lien sales only.
- Sales held annually, usually around October.
- 8% annual rate of return.
- Two years from date of sale is the redemption period.
- First to bid wins the tax lien.
- They sell over-the-counter liens, "OTC."
- Liens not sold after two years are sold as a deed.

State flag

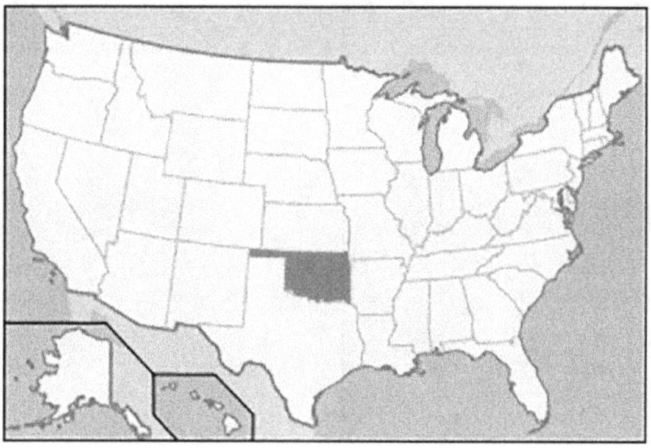

State map

Oregon

- Sold by the county, thirty-six counties.
- Tax deed sales.
- Sales held annually; varies but typically last quarter.
- No redemption period if tax deed purchased.
- No annual rate of return, you get the deed.
- Highest bid over tax lien amount wins the deed.
- Typically a 20% deposit is required for the winner.
- The county sheriff typically holds the auctions.

State flag

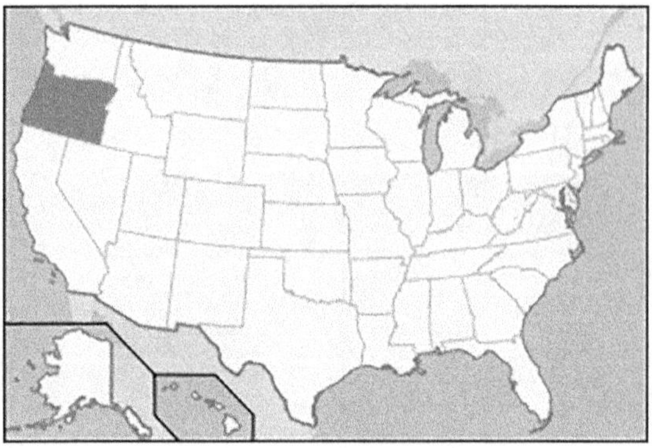

State map

Pennsylvania

- Sold by the county, sixty-four counties.
- Tax deed sales.
- Sales held year round; varies as to the dates.
- No redemption period if tax deed purchased.
- No annual rate of return, you get the deed.
- Highest bid over tax lien amount wins the deed.
- The tax collector typically holds the auctions.
- Three types of sales:
  Upset sale, subject to most liens
  Judicial sale, subject to partial liens
  Repository sale, sold free and clear

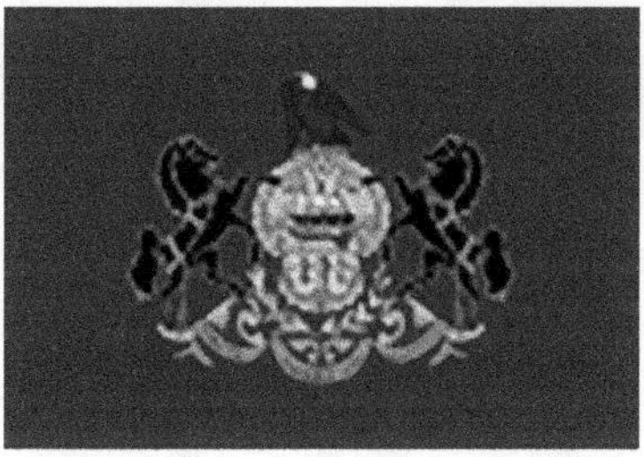

State flag

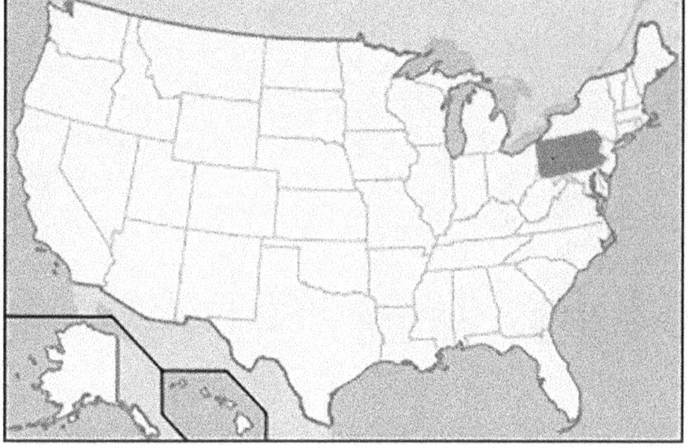

State map

Rhode Island

- Sold by the county, five counties.
- Tax deed sales.
- Sales held annually; varies as to the dates.
- One year redemption period after tax deed purchased.
- 10% interest penalty plus an additional 1% per month annual rate of return interest.
- Highest bid over tax lien amount wins the deed.
- Full amount refunded if redeemed.
- The tax collector typically holds the auctions.

State flag

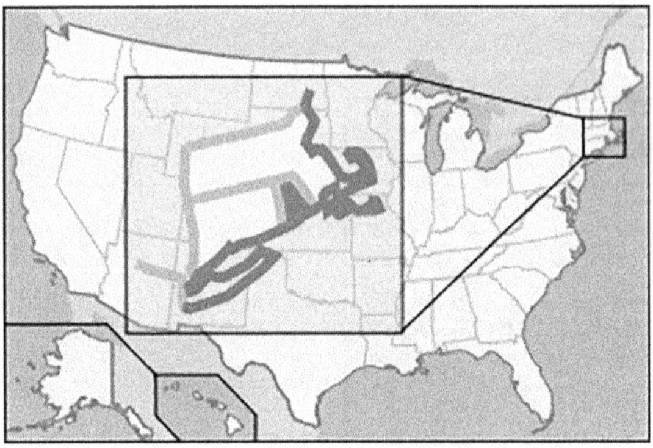

State map

South Carolina

- Sold by the county, forty-six counties.
- Tax lien sales only.
- Sales held annually, usually around October.
- 8%–12% penalty rate of return.
- Twelve to eighteen months from date of sale is the redemption period.
- Highest bid over lien amount wins the tax lien.
- You get back your premium if the lien redeems.
- They sell over-the-counter liens, "OTC."
- Deed issued after one year of purchase.

State flag

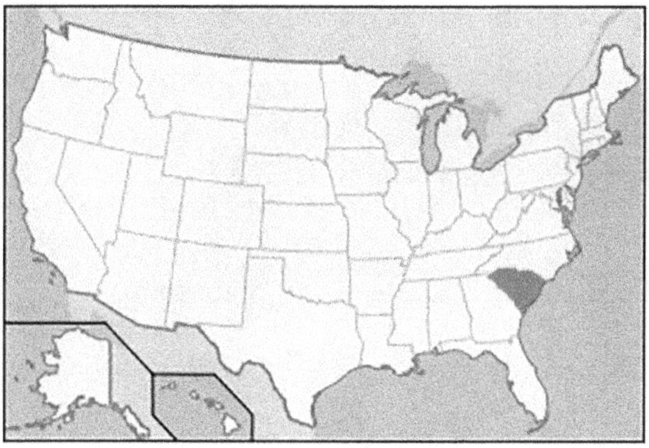

State map

South Dakota

- Sold by the county, sixty-six counties.
- Tax lien sales only.
- Sales held annually, usually around December.
- 12% annual rate of return.
- Three to four years from date of sale is the redemption period.
- Lowest interest bid wins the tax lien.
- They sell over-the-counter liens.

State flag

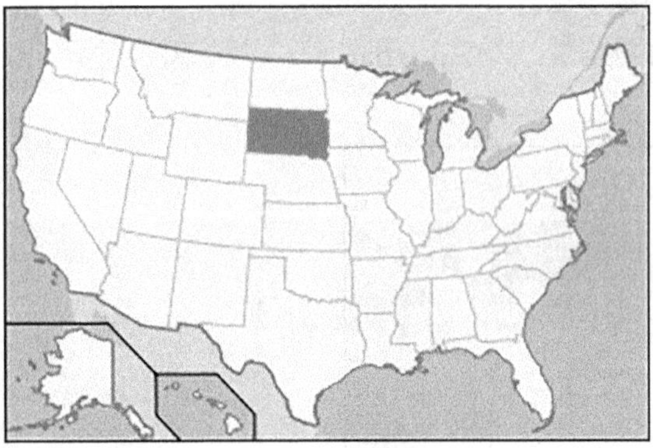

State map

Tennessee

- Sold by the county, ninety-five counties.
- Tax deed sales.
- Sales held year round; varies as to the dates.
- One year redemption period of date purchased.
- 10% annual rate of return, you get the deed.
- Highest bid over tax lien amount wins the deed.
- The tax collector typically holds the auctions.
- Yes, you get back your premium.

State flag

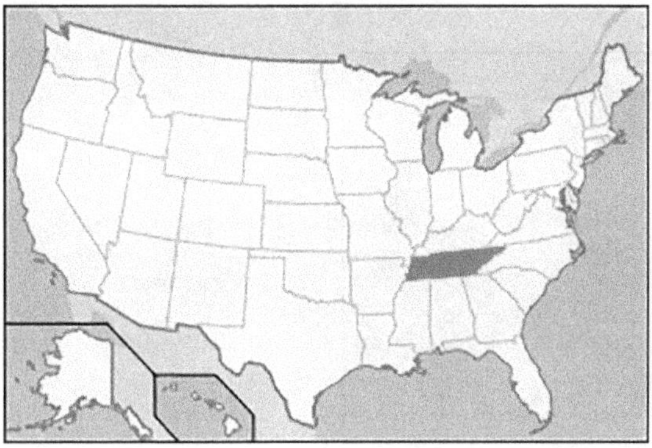

State map

Texas

- Sold by the county, 256 counties.
- Tax deed sales.
- Sales held monthly on the first Tuesday.
- Sixth months on investment property and twenty-four months on all others types are the redemption periods.
- 25% penalty interest on the deed.
- Highest bid over tax lien amount wins the deed.
- The constable typically holds the auctions.

State flag

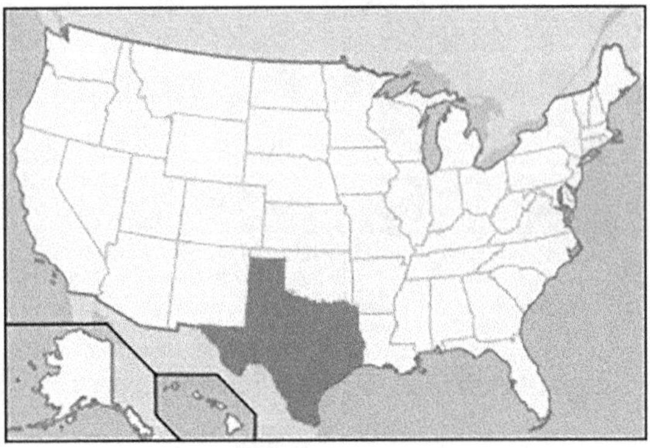

State map

Utah

- Sold by the county, twenty-nine counties.
- Tax deed sales.
- Sales held annually; varies, usually in May.
- No redemption period if tax deed purchased.
- No annual rate of return, you get the deed.
- Highest bid over tax lien amount wins the deed.
- The county auditor typically holds the auctions.

State flag

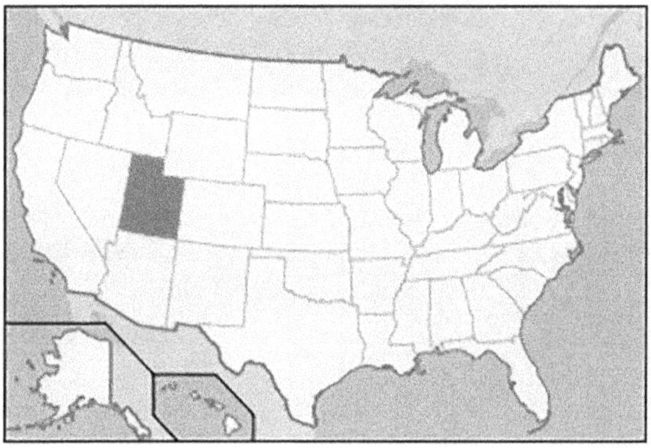

State map

Vermont

- Sold by the county, fourteen counties.
- Tax deed sales.
- Sales held year round; varies as to the dates.
- One year redemption period if tax deed purchased.
- 12% annual rate of return.
- Highest bid over tax lien amount wins the deed.
- After one year turn in tax deed for standard deed.
- The tax collector typically holds the auctions.

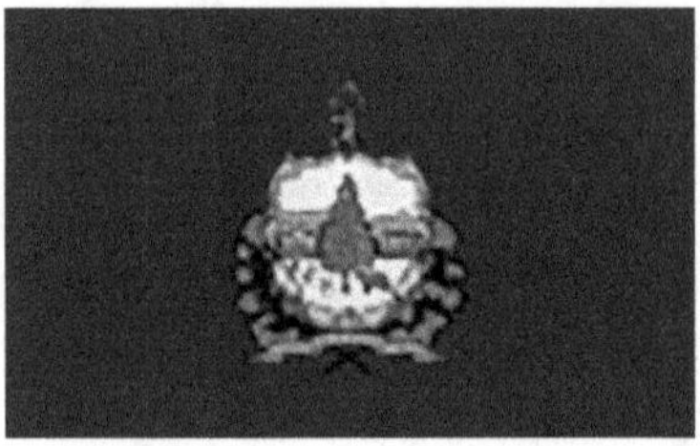

State flag

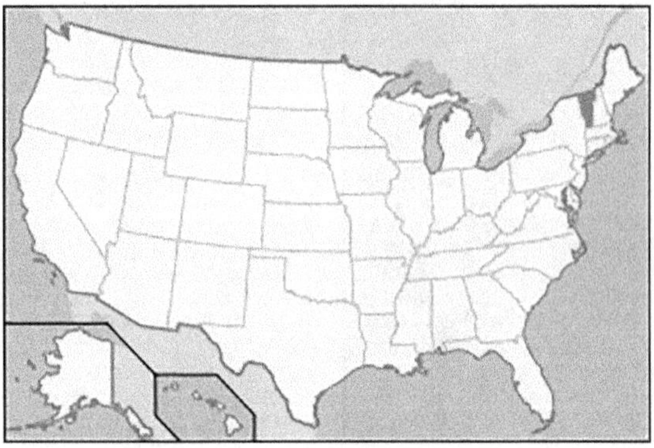

State map

Virginia

- Sold by the county, ninety-three counties.
- Tax deed sales.
- Sales held year round; usually quarterly.
- No redemption period if tax deed purchased.
- No annual rate of return, you get the deed.
- Highest bid over tax lien amount wins the deed.
- Each tax collector can set individual sale rules.
- The tax collector typically holds the auctions.

State flag

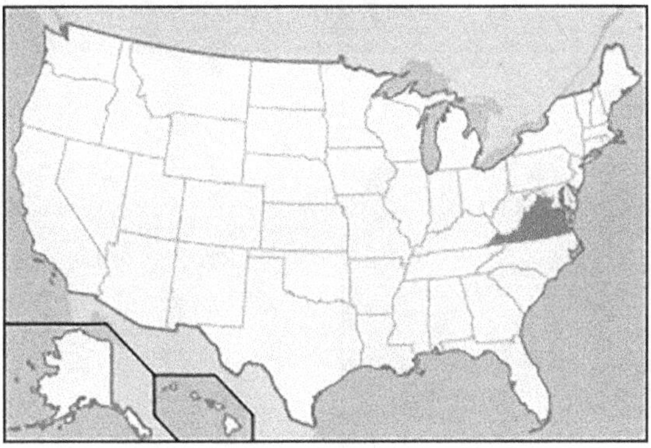

State map

Washington

- Sold by the county, thirty-nine counties.
- Tax deed sales.
- Sales held annually; varies but typically November.
- No redemption period if tax deed purchased.
- No annual rate of return, you get the deed.
- Highest bid over tax lien amount wins the deed.
- Property not sold at auction goes to the county.
- The tax collector typically holds the auctions.

State flag

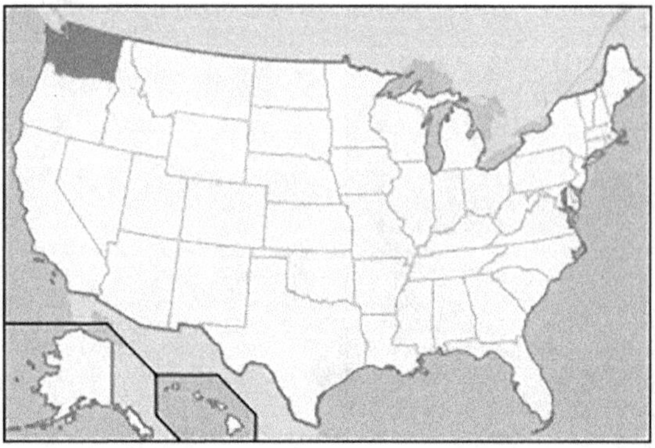

State map

West Virginia

- Sold by the county, fifty-five counties.
- Tax lien sales only.
- Sales held annually, usually around October.
- 12% annual rate of return.
- One year from date of sale is the redemption period.
- Highest bid over lien amount wins the tax lien.
- You get back your premium if the lien redeems.
- They sell over-the-counter liens.

State flag

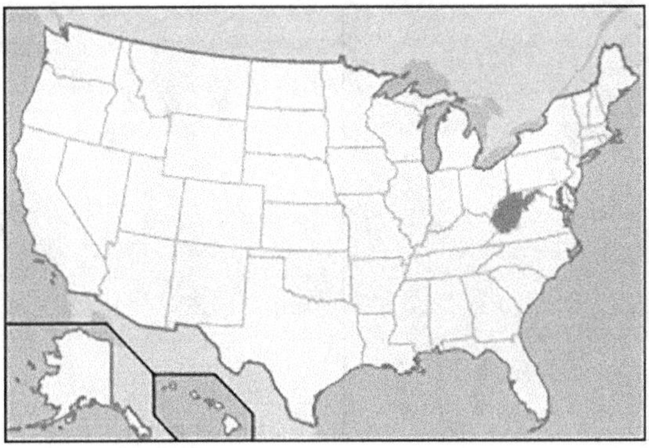

State map

Wisconsin

- Sold by the county, seventy-two counties.
- Tax deed sales.
- Sales held year round; varies as to the dates.
- No redemption period if tax deed purchased.
- No annual rate of return, you get the deed.
- Highest bid over tax lien amount wins the deed.
- The tax collector typically holds the auctions.

State flag

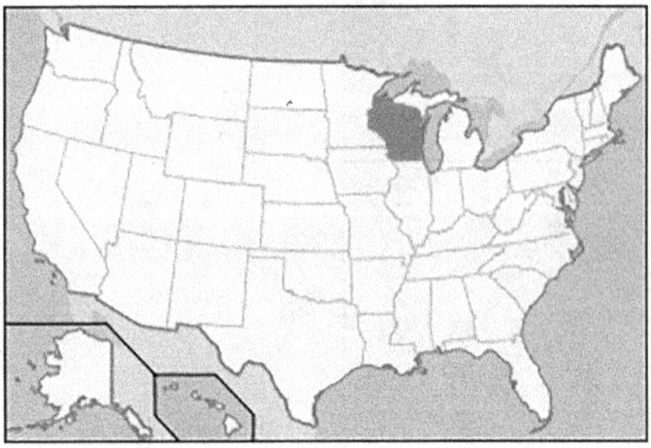

State map

Wyoming

- Sold by the county, twenty-three counties.
- Tax lien sales only.
- Sales held annually, usually between July to October.
- 15% annual rate of return.
- First year subject to a 3% penalty.
- Four years from date of sale is the redemption period.
- First to bid wins the tax lien; if there is a tie, then random drawing is done.

State flag

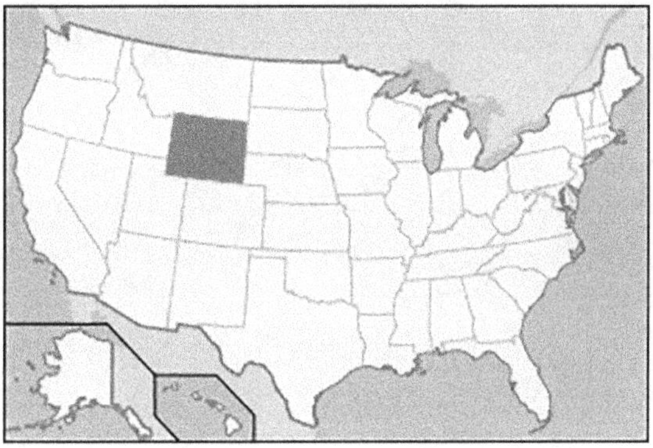

State map

Favorite Books to Read

Tax Lien$, by Michael Pellegrino, Esq
Write It Down, Make It Happen, by Henrietta Anne Klauser
Smart Couples Finish First, by David Bach
The Automatic Millionaire, by David Bach
Rich Dad Poor Dad, by Robert Kiyosaki
Cashflow Quadrant, by Robert Kiyosaki
Building Wealth, by Russ Whitney
Millionaire Mentor, by Russ Whitney
Millionaire Real Estate Mindset, by Russ Whitney

- Alabama (see title 40)
- Alaska (see title 43)
- Arizona (see title 42)
- Arkansas (see title 26)
- California (see Rev-Tax Code Part 4–7.5)
- Colorado (see title 39)
- Connecticut (see title 12)
- Delaware (see title 30)
- District of Columbia (see title 47)
- Florida (see title XIV)
- Georgia (see title 48)
- Hawaii (see title 14)
- Idaho (see title 63)
- Illinois (see chapter 35)
- Indiana (see title 6)
- Iowa (see title X)
- Kansas (see chapter 79)
- Kentucky (see title XI)
- Louisiana (searchable index)
- Maine (see title 36)
- Maryland (see Tax General/Property)
- Massachusetts (see chapters 58–65C)
- Minnesota (see chapters 270–299)
- Mississippi (see title 27)
- Missouri (see Title 10)
- Michigan (see chapters 205–211)
- Montana (see title 15)

- Nebraska (see chapter 77)
- Nevada (see title 32)
- New Hampshire (see title 5)
- New Jersey (see titles 54/54A)
- New Mexico (see chapter 7)
- New York | Alternate Site (search)
- North Carolina (see chapter 105)
- North Dakota (see title 57)
- Ohio (see title LVII)
- Oklahoma (see title 68)
- Oregon (see chapters 305–324)
- Pennsylvania (see title 72)
- Rhode Island (see title 44)
- South Carolina (see title 12)
- South Dakota (see title 10)
- Tennessee (see title 67)
- Texas (see chapter 34)
- Utah (see title 59)
- Vermont (see title 32)
- Virginia (see title 58.1)
- Washington (see titles 82–84)
- West Virginia (see chapters 11–11A)
- Wisconsin (see chapters 70–79)
- Wyoming (see title 39)

Legal disclaimer: The information in this book was taken from several sources and should not be taken as legal advice or in place of advice from your local attorney. You should still check with your tax collector as well as your real estate attorney in the county in which you will invest in tax liens and tax deeds.

Specific State Information

Alabama

- Tax lien sales.
- Sales held annually, usually around May.
- 12% annual rate of return.
- Three years from the date of sale is the redemption period.
- Highest bid over lien amount wins.
- Yes, you get back your premium.
- They sell over-the-counter liens.

Alaska

- Tax deed sales.
- Sales held year round.
- No redemption period.
- Highest bid over lien amount wins.

Arizona

- Tax lien sales.
- Sales held annually, usually around February.
- 16% annual rate of return.
- Three years from the date of sale is the redemption period.
- Lowest bid o for interest rate wins.
- They sell over-the-counter liens.

Arkansas

- Tax deed sales.
- Sales held quarterly.
- Thirty days from the date of sale is the redemption period.
- Highest bid over lien amount wins.
- They sell over-the-counter liens.

California

- Tax deed sales.
- Sales held year round.
- Highest bid over lien amount wins.

Colorado

- Tax lien sales.
- Sales held annually, usually between October and December.
- Nine points above fed discount rate as set in September is the annual percent rate of return.
- Three years from the date of sale is the redemption period.
- Highest bid over lien amount wins.
- You do *not* get back your premium.

- They sell over-the-counter liens.

Connecticut
- Tax deed sales with redemption.
- Sales held year round.
- 18% annual rate of return.
- One year from the date of sale is the redemption period.
- Highest bid over lien amount wins.
- Yes, you get back your premium.

Delaware
- Tax deed sales with redemption.
- Sales held monthly.
- 15% of bid amount rate of return.
- Sixty days from the date of sale is the redemption period.
- Highest bid over lien amount wins.

District of Columbia
- Tax lien.
- Sales held annually, usually the third Tuesday of July.
- 1.5% per month rate of return.
- Six months from the date of sale is the redemption period.
- Highest bid over lien amount wins.
- Yes, you get back your premium.
- They do not sell over-the-counter liens.

Florida
- Tax lien.
- Sales held annually, usually between April and June.
- 18% rate of return.
- Two years from the date of sale is the redemption period.
- Lowest interest rate bid for lien wins.
- They sell over-the-counter liens.

Florida

- Tax deed sales
- Sales held monthly.
- No redemption period.
- Highest bid over lien amount wins.

Georgia

- Tax deed sales with redemption.
- Sales held monthly.
- 20% penalty rate of return.
- One year from the date of sale is the redemption period.
- Highest bid over lien amount wins.
- Yes, you get back your premium.

Hawaii

- Tax deed sales with redemption.
- Sales held year round, usually in the spring.
- 12% annual rate of return for first year.
- Redemption period is one year from the date of recording deed.
- Highest bid over lien amount wins.
- Yes, you get back your premium.

Idaho

- Tax deed sales.
- Sales held year round.
- No redemption period.
- Highest bid over lien amount wins.

Illinois

- Tax lien.
- Sales held annually, usually between October and November.
- 18% rate of return.
- Two years from the date of sale is the redemption period.
- Lowest bid on interest rate amount wins.

Indiana

- Tax lien.
- Sales held annually, usually between September and October.
- If held < six months = 10%/> six months < one year = 15%/> one year = 25% penalty rate of return.
- One year from the date of sale is the redemption period.
- Highest bid over lien amount wins.
- Yes, you get back your premium.

Iowa

- Tax lien sale.
- Sales held annually, usually around the third Monday of June.
- 24% rate of return.
- Twenty-one months from the date of sale is the redemption period.
- Lowest bid on interest rate on lien wins.

Kansas

- Tax deed sales.
- Sales held year round.
- No redemption period.
- Highest bid over lien amount wins.

Kentucky

- Tax lien sale.
- Sales held annually.
- 12% rate of return.
- One year from the date of sale is the redemption period.
- First to bid wins.

Louisiana

- Tax lien.
- Sales held annually, usually between May and June.

- 5% plus 1% per month first year, then 12 % percent rate of return.
- Three years from the date of sale is the redemption period.
- Lowest percent of ownership wins.

Maine

- Tax deed sales.
- Sales held year round.
- No redemption period.
- Highest bid over lien amount wins.

Maryland

- Tax lien sale.
- Sales held annually, usually between May and June.
- 6–14 % rate of return depending on county.
- Six months from the date of sale is the redemption period.
- Highest bid over lien amount wins.
- Yes, you get back your premium.

Massachusetts

- Tax lien sales.
- Counties usually take these liens to foreclosure.
- Tax deed sales.
- Sales held annually.
- 16% annual rate of return.
- Upon completion of a quiet title suit is the redemption period.
- Highest bid wins.
- Yes, you get back your premium.

Michigan

- Tax deed sales.
- Sales held year round.
- No redemption period.
- Highest bid over lien amount wins.

Minnesota

- Tax deed sales.
- Sales held year round.
- No redemption period.
- Highest bid over lien amount wins.
- The sell over-the-counter liens.

Mississippi

- Tax lien sales.
- Sales held annually, usually around April and August.
- 12 % to 18% annual rate of return depending on the county.
- Two years from the date of sale is the redemption period.
- Highest bid over lien amount wins.
- Yes, you get back your premium.

Missouri

- Tax lien.
- Sales held annually, usually around fourth Monday in August.
- 10% rate of return.
- One year from the date of sale is the redemption period.
- Highest bid over lien amount wins.
- Yes, you get back your premium.
- They sell over-the-counter liens.

Montana

- Tax lien sales held annually, usually around June or July.
- 10% rate of return.
- Three years (buildings) and two years (land) from the date of sale are the redemption periods.
- First to offer minimum bid wins.
- They sell over-the-counter liens.

Nebraska

- Tax lien.

- Sales held annually, usually around March and April.
- 3% over fed discount rate in July of previous year is the rate of return.
- Two years from the date of sale is the redemption period.
- Rotational bid wins.
- You do *not* get back your premium.
- They sell over-the-counter liens.

Nevada

- Tax lien sales (on special assessments only).
- Sales held annually, usually around April.
- Three years from the date of sale is the redemption period.
- Highest bid over lien amount or lottery bid wins.
- They sell over-the-counter liens.
- Tax deed sales
- Sales held annually.
- No redemption period after the sale.
- Highest bid over lien amount wins.
- Yes, you get back your premium.

New Hampshire

- Tax lien sales (county only).
- Tax deed sales.
- Sales held annually.
- 18% rate of return.
- Two years from the date of sale is the redemption period.
- Highest bid over lien amount wins.
- You do not get back your premium.

New Jersey

- Tax lien sales.
- Sales held usually.
- 18% rate of return.
- Two years from the date of sale is the redemption period.
- Lowest interest rate bid on lien wins.

- Yes, you get back your premium if not longer than five years.
- They sell over-the-counter liens.

New Mexico
- Tax deed sales.
- Sales held year round.
- No redemption period.
- Highest bid over lien amount wins.

New York
- Tax lien sales.
- Sales held usually.
- Tax deed sales.
- Sales held annually.
- No redemption period.
- Highest bid over lien amount wins.

North Carolina
- Tax deed sales.
- Sales held year round, usually on Mondays.
- No redemption period.
- Highest bid over lien amount wins, subject to upset bids.
- Yes, you get back your premium.

North Dakota
- Tax deed sales.
- Sales held year round, around November and December.
- No redemption period.
- Highest bid over lien amount wins.

Ohio
- Tax lien sales.
- Sales held annually.
- 18% rate of return.

- One year from the date of sale is the redemption period.
- Highest bid over lien amount wins.
- Yes, you get back your premium.

Ohio
- Tax deed sales.
- Sales held monthly.
- Highest bid over lien amount wins.

Oklahoma
- Tax lien sales.
- Sales held annually, usually around October.
- 8% rate of return.
- Two years from the date of sale is the redemption period.
- First to bid lien amount wins.
- They sell over-the-counter liens.

Oregon
- Tax deed sales with redemption.
- Sales held annually.
- 20% of purchase price interest.
- 120 days from date of sale is the redemption period.
- Highest bid over the lien wins.

Pennsylvania
- Tax deed sales.
- Sales held annually.
- No redemption period.
- Highest bid over lien amount wins.
- They sell over-the-counter liens.

Rhode Island
- Tax deed sales with redemption.
- Sales held annually, usually around June.
- One year from date of sale is the redemption period.

- Lowest percent of ownership bid wins.

South Carolina

- Tax lien sales.
- Sales held annually, usually around October to December.
- 3% penalty quarterly.
- One year from the date of sale is the redemption period.
- Highest bid over lien amount wins.
- Yes, you get back your premium.

South Dakota

- Tax lien sales.
- Sales held annually, usually around the third Monday in December.
- 12% rate of return.
- Three to four years from the date of sale is the redemption period based on the county.
- Lowest interest rate bid on lien wins.
- They sell over-the-counter liens.

Tennessee

- Tax deed sales with redemption.
- Sales held annually.
- One year from date of sale is the redemption period.
- Highest bid over lien amount wins.
- Yes, you get back your premium.

Texas

- Tax deed sales with redemption.
- Sales held monthly.
- 25% penalty interest investments for first six months.
- 25% per year penalty interest homestead and ranches first two years.
- Six months to 2 years is the redemption period.
- Highest bid over lien amount wins.

- Yes, you get back your premium.
- They sell over-the-counter liens.

Utah

- Tax deed sales.
- Sales held annually.
- No redemption period.
- Highest bid over lien amount wins.
- They sell over-the-counter liens.

Vermont

- Tax deed sales with redemption.
- Sales held monthly.
- 12% interest on tax lien.
- One year is the redemption period.
- Highest bid over lien amount wins.
- Yes, you get back your premium.

Virginia

- Tax deed sales.
- Sales held annually.
- No redemption period.
- Highest bid over lien amount wins.

Washington

- Tax deed sales with redemption.
- Sales held annually, around November and December.
- Highest bid over lien amount wins.
- Yes, you get back your premium.
- One year right of redemption by owner.

West Virginia

- Tax lien sales.
- Sales held usually, between October and November.
- 12% rate of return.

- One year from the date of sale is the redemption period.
- Highest bid over lien amount wins.
- Yes, you get back your premium.
- They sell over-the-counter liens.

Wisconsin

- Tax deed sales.
- Sales held annually.
- No redemption period.
- Highest bid over lien amount wins.

Wyoming

- Tax lien sales.
- Sales held annually, usually between July and October.
- 15% (plus 3% penalty first year only) rate of return.
- Four years from the date of sale is the redemption period.
- First to offer lien amount wins, if a tie occurs, then random drawing shall be done.

Top Six Tax Lien/Deed Holders in the United States

American Tax Funding, LLC
630 US Highway One, Suite 300
North Palm Beach, Florida 33408
www.atfs.com

Bankers Trust Company
4 Albany Street
New York, NY10006

MD Sass
Avenue of the Americas
New York, NY
www.mdsass.com

Breen Capital
101 Farnsworth Avenue
Bordentown, NJ 08505

Crusader Servicing Corp. 6526 Castor Avenue
Philadelphia, Pa. 19149

Plymouth Financial
1-800-575-9890
www.plymouthfinancial.com

Mooring Financial
Lambert
www.mooringfinancial.com

www.taxserve.com

www.carc.com

Terms

Assignment of tax liens: These are tax liens that were sold at the sale and were then sold by way of an assignment to another party. They can be purchased directly from the taxing jurisdiction and usually earn the maximum interest rate available or from original tax lien holder at the rate of interest won at the sale. Usually, they can be purchased by mail.

Bid: The manner in which a person makes an offer to purchase.

Block and lot: A method in which the taxing authority can identify a piece of property.

Court action: A proceeding in a court where a plaintiff makes a claim against a defendant.

Deed: A written document used to convey title to a piece of property.

Deed of trust: A document used in some states in lieu of a mortgage.

Foreclosure of a tax lien: The process of enforcing a lien against property for nonpayment of delinquent property taxes. Taxing authorities hold a superior lien against all taxable property to enforce the payment of their taxes.

Judgment of foreclosure and sale: Order signed by the judge directing a notice of sale to be published and the referee to sell a property at auction. Also ratifies amount of money owed to lender.

Judicial foreclosure state: State where foreclosure proceeding must go through the court before a property can be sold at auction.

Lis pendens: Recorded notice of filing a legal action for nonpayment of taxes. It can also be used for nonpayment of a mortgage.

Notice of sale: A communication notice to the general public of the intent to sell a property at a foreclosure auction.

OTC liens (over the counter): The downside is they are the parcels that nobody wanted to buy at the sale.

Official lists: This is the list the taxing jurisdiction publishes. We will include the information that the taxing jurisdiction included with the exception of photographs and long legal descriptions if the parcel number or some other method of identifying the parcel is given.

Overbid: The amount of the winning bid that exceeds the amount of taxes owed.

Redeemable deed sales: This is a sale that is called a tax deed sale, but the sale is subject to a right of redemption during a specified time period by the delinquent property owner. For most purposes, the sale is very similar to a tax lien sale.

Redemption rights: The individual property owner of subsequent tax lien holder's right to satisfy the outstanding tax lien.

Tax deed sale: A tax deed sale gives the buyer immediate ownership of the property. This ownership often requires the filing of a quiet title action to have marketable title, but it is not subject to redemption by the delinquent tax payer.

Tax-defaulted land sale: These are lands that have gone through a sale and were not purchased by a tax sale buyer. They instead were purchased by the taxing jurisdiction or the state and are not available for purchase on a negotiated purchase.

Tax lien: A debt attached to a property for nonpayment of taxes.

Tax lien certificate: A document used to show the ownership of a tax lien that was sold.

Tax lien sale: A tax lien sale does not give the lien buyer ownership of the property. It gives the buyer a claim for money that is superior to almost all other liens, including mortgages, and is secured by the real estate. If this claim for money is not satisfied, the lien holder can apply for and receive the property, subject to the conditions set by the statutes for the jurisdiction. Approximate redemption rate for residential properties is somewhat above 90% in most jurisdictions.

Tax taking: The taxing jurisdiction "takes" the property and becomes the owner. The property is later sold, either through a negotiated sale or an auction.

About the Author

After an honorable discharge from USMC as a Second Lieutenant, Thomas settled down, and he and his wife, Cindy, have five children and two granddaughters. His journey from military life to construction general contracting was an easy transition based on his family and faith in God. Serving others has been the path Thomas has taken from remodeling homes to performing inspections or as a minister of Holy Communion at St. Andrew Catholic Church.

As a member of the local Knights of Columbus, Council 7131, in Cape Coral, and having served as the Grand Knight, placing others first and treating them as he would be treated have been the guiding light of his life. His personal and business motto, "People before profits," has served him well as he personally trained others to benefit from his knowledge and success in real estate.

In 2001, he became and national trainer and mentor to guide individuals in the art of creating financial security by investing safely in real estate to permit them to reach financial independence. Thomas expanded into the international arena to train and mentor individuals and has spoken to groups from forty-five attendees to over four thousand.

Thomas is an active investor and participates in weekly tax deed auctions in Florida. Thomas is also the CEO and founder of TLD International, LLC, and Claire Bancale & Associates for purchasing tax liens, tax deeds and direct purchases.

Cindy and Thomas now look to use their skills to develop property acquired at the tax lien and deed sales to provide affordable quality housing to veterans, first responders and educators.

CPSIA information can be obtained
at www.ICGtesting.com
Printed in the USA
BVHW041930250220
573286BV00011B/134

9 781098 006044